SMALL BUSINESS IDEAS

DO WHAT YOU LOVE AND MAKE MONEY ONLINE WITH AMAZON FBA, BLOGGING, SOCIAL MEDIA, AND MORE!

JACQUELINE CONSON

TABLE OF CONTENTS

CHAPTER ONE 6

INTRODUCTION 6

CHAPTER TWO 13

BLOGGING 13

- 15
- What Is Blogging About? 15
- Rules of Conduct 16
- How to Decide What to Blog On 18
- How to Start A Wordpress Blog 20
- 5 Easy Steps to Designing a Blog Logo 22
- Getting Your Blog Launched 25

CHAPTER THREE 28

FREELANCE WRITING 28

- Six Tips For A Powerful Freelance Writing Career 29
- How to Start a Freelance Website 32
- 10 Steps The Way to Begin a Freelancing Business While Working Full-Time in 2020 (and Why You Should) 38
- Should You Start a Freelance Business While Working Full-Time? 50

CHAPTER FOUR 55

AFFILIATE ADVERTISING 55

- Affiliate Network Marketing Risk: 60
- Exclusive Affiliate community Campaign Benefits: 61
- Launching affiliate advertising campaigns which Combine: 62
- How to Start 63

CHAPTER FIVE 76

AMAZON FBA 76

- Construction 78
- The Way to Make It Yourself 79
- How you do this would be to create as much use of their accessible content area as you can. 81
- How to Start 83
- Utilizing Merchant Words, Jungle Scout and Much Keyword Tools 86
- Organizing Your Brand 90
- Compose Your Merchandise 93
- Fill In All Of The Appropriate Info 95

CHAPTER SIX 101

MAKE MONEY ON YOUTUBE 101

- Measures on how to Earn Money on YouTube 101
- What's YouTube Affiliate Marketing? 107

CHAPTER SEVEN 108

EBAY DROPSHIPPING 108

- What's Dropshipping? 108
- How Can Dropship on eBay Work? 108
- Dropshipping on eBay: Pros and Cons 109
- 8 Tips on eBay Dropshipping 111
- The best way to Dropship on eBay: A Step-by-Step Guide 116

CHAPTER EIGHT 118

FLIX ANF FLIP HOUSES 119

- What's House Flipping? 120
- 121
- The way to spin a Home in 5 Easy Steps 121

CHAPTER NINE 126

INSTAGRAM AGENCY 126

- How to Create a Style Guide for Your Website (Free Worksheets!) 127

CHAPTER TEN 128

SOCIAL MEDIA MANAGEMENT 128

- Social Media Management Tools 129
- The Vital Elements of Social Media Management 130
- Price of Social Media Management Tools 131

CHAPTER ELEVEN 133

MISTAKES TO PREVENT 133

- Starting a Company That You Are Not Passionate About 133
- Selecting a Niche, That's Too Narrow 138

CHAPTER TWELVE 141

SUMMARY 141

CHAPTER ONE
INTRODUCTION

For two decades, the international internet has continued to establish itself as a viable tool for constructing, managing, and creating a corporation. Little doubt remains that you might earn money on the internet and discover success by doing this. In fact, since starting our very own online jobs, we've had the possibility of working and meeting with several unique individual entrepreneurs who, like you, talk about a fantasy of finding economic freedom by running their businesses. Since you may have guessed, a few found success online.

The Worldwide web provides not merely a valid source for beginning your own company, which delivers a reliable supply of income to loved ones but a virtually infinite supply of ideas and opportunities to market and develop your company. It may even supply you with all the flexibility to operate at house, freedom to function part-time, or the capacity to create an additional source of income that would make your life more gratifying.

Now we would love to discuss with all the wisdom and resources we picked up along the way and offer you a couple of shortcuts to help enhance your internet tasks.

Starting a web company and becoming financially individual is presently a realistic proposal for anyone that has a computer and net access. Of the many unique methods to start doing so, some might offer a great return for the attempts, but sadly, several internet companies don't triumph, and people working them fail to create enough to make it worthwhile.

There are numerous instances where someone has written an eBook and published it, or opened up on an online retail shop, eventually to discover there aren't any buyers that the sole means to earn money everywhere would be to get paying clients; the proposal is the perfect method to receive them. You can find a couple of wonderful techniques that drive visitors or customers to your site, so this novel is all about successful proven approaches that you could use to construct a lasting passive income online. Some of the things which worked a couple of years ago are not viable now because the World Wide Web is always changing, growing, and evolving every day. With 3.5 billion existing clients using the internet every day and yet another 3 billion potential clients in Africa, India, China, and the rest of Asia, the sky is the limit for new companies and also an infinite earnings supply. Now is the ideal time to grab the so-called "gravy train," however, you will need people, quality content, and also to be prepared to perform the important jobs (often quite a great deal of project). But only doing the task is no guarantee of success, so you still have to be functioning in the Ideal Places and performing the Ideal things, then living on a "passive income" since it is known as the phrase currently used to refer to this income individuals receive over the net. It is known as passive income since, in concept, the vast majority of the job must be completed, and then you settle back and reap the rewards of your labor with minimal labor involved. In practice, some other internet company will require continuing maintenance; the sum required relies on the site; its application as well as the product you're providing. You'll find many distinct manners of internet companies that range from those that require a daily input, and the ones set completely automated.

Some Online businesses are practical and practical approaches to create money on the internet. A lot of individuals have composed some initial intellectual property, like an eBook, an internet class, site posts, or similar, then set up an online shop to market their merchandise. Whether they are created or made from your operator, or acquired from other sources, then there is a considerable quantity of electricity and time needed to prepare the site and personalize it. After this is finished and your site has gone, then you will have to carry out various marketing tasks like promoting your site or articles and interacting with individuals on social networking.

Finding similar sites or websites and providing quality feedback and remarks is a great way to promote your website provided that it's attained in a specific manner. A fantastic blog or website has new excellent content regularly contained to encourage visitors to go back, not only preloaded with posts, and also made to stagnate. A good deal of the stuff on a website or blog may come from somebody else you employ to write the article for you. However, you are the person who has to edit the program and handle the entire operation. Each one of these items isn't passive at every one of the profits, if any, can be very allusive in case you are not careful.

There are scores and scores of schemes that pop up all the time. They generally stick to precisely the identical routine or similar rag to riches "Cinderella Story," where this person was on the verge of bankruptcy or committing suicide because they were so distressed. Next, as a result of the love of the Loved Ones or their pup, they chose to offer that the World Wide Web is just one final shot, and they stumbled upon somebody who, for whatever reason, gave them a minute formula to make fantastic sums. They make a 6-figure income functioning less than one hour daily while sitting in their beach amid private heaven they paid for in cash after just one year of utilizing this formulation. They would like to go back and are supplying this information free to you in case you connect with not $1200, or $600, or even $100. It's yours today just and for specially chosen people at the current spot price of $9.99, but hurry this deal is limited.

Or some dribble is simply going to earn money for the man or woman who's selling the plan. If you would like to select some moment, do have the capability to create a dream very similar to the one over, it's a sensible approach to produce a passive income for just a little while, even though you have to live with yourself knowing that you are simply ripping off individuals (typically desperate women and men that aren't able to manage it).

There's no doubt that a few folks would make a simple buck on the net, but the majority of people will fight at least originally, precisely finding it hard to create as you want if you had a normal occupation, however, if you're all set to spend time and energy required. It's a very nice and sound system to provide lasting long-term earnings.

Building solid long-term passive income online demands several matters; the main is getting visitors. Traffic is the term used to describe individuals coming or visiting your website. It is an easy formula: the men and women who visit your site, the more money you're going to be able to make, no visitors, no cash, full stop. It isn't important how good or how cheap your product or service deal is, even if there's not anybody to view it, therefore nobody can buy it. The next very important problem is acquiring something other folks needed, which they are ready to pay you to get it. The upcoming important issue is your credibility online. This, for instance, individuals, can take a while to accumulate; nevertheless, there are many methods to speed up this.

It is possible to obtain a mailing list off the net using hundreds and sometimes thousands of mail addresses; nevertheless, these are often of small value for many aspects. These documents are obsolete and are utilized by several folks to try and advertise their things, so the answer level is extremely low. Another reason why these lists are of dubious worth is that you are better at trying to become superior results of people who have lent an interest in everything you're providing rather than simply shooting emails, which will result in many people's spam or junk mail files if it gets past their spam blockers.

The Expression "e-Business" may be used regularly; nonetheless, e-Business means different things to various women and men. To some people, e-Business is just employing a website utilizing a toll-free amount of individuals who may call to place an order. Other women and men think e-Business is employing an internet site that permits clients to release their credit card info on the internet, though their requests may subsequently be processed manually precisely like a fax or phone order. Others think that e-Business means using the capability to place a safe online purchase, using immediate charge card confirmation, and utilizing a fully integrated backend database that automatically opens and informs the customer of the most recent costs and if an item is currently in stock. The goal is, the way you specify e-Business and the way you employ e-Business on your site depends on your company and the type of product or services you're promoting online.

For Example, a program development company that offers a downloadable program software (i.e., does not have any actual boxed version) has no inventory. Hence, they wouldn't call for a backend inventory database to be integrated using their e-Business system. All they may require is your e-Business system, which validates credit card information and requires payment. On the other hand, if you have an internet business that intends to market novels, and you need to become the next Amazon.com, then you will require a full size, complete-featured, fully incorporated e-Business approach to competing with all the Amazon.com of the planet. Otherwise, prospective customers can store at Amazon.com because their e-Business process is a lot more convenient and simple to use.

The demographics and dimensions of the online people, which constitute the online world is a significant element of the business as each firm should have a thorough understanding of the target market to be lucrative. Typically, the sum of internet users is increasing at a staggering speed. The Computer Industry Almanac has noted that from the calendar year 2002, 490 million individuals throughout the globe may have Internet accessibility; that is 79.4 per 1,000 people internationally, and 118 people per 1,000 by the year 2005. There are now 374.9 million internet users worldwide. From a demographics perspective, Internet clients are generally well educated, technically aggressively, and financially well off. Popular applications of this Web are for research purposes, entertainment, email, chat, and also online shopping as the net expands to does the wide variety of opportunities for companies.

The Web was called a market comprising mostly young, professional men. Within 2000, we found the demographics which constitute the internet universe diversify and enlarge. Shifts in Internet demographics are all called to continue in the long run because the usage of the Internet continues to become a recognized part of daily life. The first quarter of 2000 marked the first time the number of women online in the United States supersedes that of men, according to a report by Media Metrix and Jupiter Communications. The number of seniors on the World Wide Web is one of the most fast-growing parts of the World Wide Web. The quantity of seniors online on the day has been projected at over 23 million based on a variety of sources. IDC, a leading industry analyst, also expects the number of seniors on the internet to increase into 34.1 million by 2004, an estimated 20% of new users.
Along with the rise in the number of seniors occurring to the online world, you may observe again the number of possibilities available to companies that target this section. Recent surveys from Harris Interactive found that "young people" from the U.S. between the

ages of 18 and 24 have a significant quantity of buying power, and are investing at an estimated $164 billion annually. This signifies an appealing section for businesses because a good portion of the $164 billion is spent on the internet, and e-Business spending among this age group is significantly more than four times the speed of e-Business paying among adults.

E-Business brings forth a range of valuable opportunities for existing businesses and fresh start-ups alike. Does this open up the doors to new markets, but additionally, it can open up the doorway to new market opportunities. Think about the travel industry. Traditionally clients would assess their travel broker for holiday packages and airport details. The advent of the World Wide Web and e-Business altered the principles for the travel business, and also new businesses including Travelocity.com and Expedia.com was able to enter to the highly competitive marketplace by giving rock bottom prices and empowering the consumer with the capacity to swiftly and easily organize their excursions without interacting using a traveling agent. These new companies could provide their solutions into a massive market and at a much lower price than could conventional travel brokers at the time; consequently, they have been very profitable. This is just 1 example of how firms can attain success via e-Business.

The Internet expansion into each company and personal communications is inevitable. What has been considered a "fashion" has become the "norm." As people are becoming more comfortable and anticipating line transactions, the customer connection was improved each month due to new security-based technologies are being manufactured. New media support classes may also be speeding up the learning curve of ordinary users.

The future is bright for e-Businesses. Not everything is on the net yet. Hot items available online have always been around and are still apparel, computer hardware/software, tunes, books, toys, and travel; however, a growing number of individuals are thinking up new business ideas every day to meet clients' needs and adjustments in the online demographics. A recent survey conducted by Roper Starch discovered that Internet consumers are getting to be a lot more receptive to utilizing the World Wide Web to conduct private business, including banking, in addition to purchasing online. According to the research, in 1998, 31 percent of individuals surveyed shopped online, 16% conducted private banking online, together with 11% traded stocks. In 2000, each one of these figures climbed to 56 percent, 25%, and 16% respectively. Many studies suggest these amounts will continue growing during the upcoming few years, demonstrating many opportunities to companies trying to expand their operations online. Connected into this B2B (Business to Business) market, the Yankee Group estimates that 90 percent of small, medium-sized businesses make at least one purchase online annually.

Online Earnings was predicted to rise to $3.2 billion by 2004, according to Forrester Research. These are encouraging numbers, however, for dot com businesses, the calendar year, 2000, was filled up with a variety of tough challenges. No more can an e-Business triumph based on a great idea you desire the perfect e-Business version, the perfect online site, and also the ideal quantity of targeted traffic. This year you will see e-Business proceed from having an alternative to a regular part of several businesses daily operations it's already begun.Com or a mortar and bricks, a recognized business or your organization, is simply a dream; this novel is going to help you in getting your business online and serve as a manual on the road to e-Business Success.

This Publication will explore specific procedures for creating a long-term passive income. It will notify you of a few of the positive and negative points, benefits, and drawbacks, so you're able to generate an educated decision about the best way for one to proceed.

CHAPTER TWO
BLOGGING

What is a blog and what does a site stand for are two different questions that many Net users still ask often. Well, in short, a blog is essentially an online journal where a blogger or even a contributor to a blog can note their thoughts, ideas, opinions and practically anything else which bloggers want people to see.

Websites are often known as weblogs since, after all, they are a particular type of site, usually maintained and upgraded by an individual with regular entrances of events, descriptions of scenarios, personal commentaries, or other material such as picture images or movie. Entries are, more frequently than not, displayed in reverse-chronological purchase.

Websites are fluid, interactive platforms for authors to get their message across to subscribers, rather than a more static site platform.

There are many tools available on the World Wide Web to supply you with Blogging tips and data. For instance, should you create your site utilizing a blogging system like blogger.com or purchase your domain name and put up your site via a platform like Word Press. One significant part of preparing your blog is that it enables the blogger to develop a bond with their readers and also to have the ability to interact together. It is a great way to make your ideas known to other people, to pass on valuable information to interested readers, or to create a web presence for your company. The choices are numerous.

It's a good idea to add an "About Us" type page, where the website owner can outline who they are and disclose the objective of the blog to their subscribers or visitors.

Therefore, that, in the primary, the blogger wants to know the subject well enough to compose regular blog articles. I say "in the primary" because the versatility of a website will allow the blogger to compose a post encouraging their readers to comment on a subject that is not so well known by the blogger.

This strategy will further enhance the bloggers' bond with the readers and provides fresher, unique content to their blog.

As stated above, blog posts need to be made regularly, but not overly regular if the standard of the blog posts is of bad quality. For instance, it is much better to post only one quite informative, quality website post every 2 or 3 days rather than several flimsy posts daily. In summary, it's the caliber of the article in place of the quantity. Posting poor excellent posts too frequently will drive your readers away.

Very often forgotten by bloggers is the need to add tags in their blog posts. Tags let you target your articles into various classes, which could then be hunted by readers. For each of your posts, you ought to be seeking to have two or three tags. Make use of tags properly. By way of example, ensure you use the exact phrases for similar articles but do not give articles a lot of tags because this tends to clog up categories.

Do not have a lot of widgets or images on your site to the extent it slows down the loading of your blog. Clients will exit very quickly in the event the site takes too long to load.

Always remember also that blogs and blog posting ought to be enjoyable. It is not like writing articles for article directories. A blog article should be written more like your personal experiences as opposed to a regurgitation of a load of researched info. For instance, one of my passions is soccer. If I had been posting a blog post on a soccer match, then I would write it based on my own experiences of attending a soccer match instead of spouting a load of advice about exactly what a soccer match is - principles, time a game lasts for, etc..

The versatility of a website enables the visitor to get their message across and also to take on board any replies or feedback from their viewers. It does not take that long to establish a site - many strategies and guidelines can be found on the internet.

-

- **What Is Blogging About?**

The answer to this issue is indeed simple, but only if you understand its significance. Blog stands for weblog, which is a kind of online service. People who write blogs are known as bloggers. It offers an opportunity for bloggers to post content online, which is usually theme-based. It can be thought of as a diary where you can compose your views. They are inversely in chronological order. They were initially launched in the 1990s, and also they gained immense recognition in 2004. It is a sort of social networking website which the bloggers may use to their personal or professional purpose. Some publishers use their sites to market and publish their books. The books that are printed using blogs are called "Blooks."

Different Types Of Blogs Are Given Below:

Blogs are of two types. The first kind of site is private Blogs, where the writers write a few of their life's important events. The second type of blog is the corporation or organizational sites. Organizational blogs are largely utilized for advertising purposes. Organizational writers are usually businessmen, servicemen, etc. They want to promote their merchandise and maintain their audiences updated on various business events occurring. They're also able to use their blogs for advertising customers or sales opinions. This would be to assist folks read about a specific product before they buy it.

Personal blogs are mostly utilized to upgrade the writers' household members, friends, and relatives about the latest events going on in their lives. Some individuals also use personal blogs to vent their frustration by simply expressing their feelings and ideas.

- **Rules of Conduct**

  - You'll be responsible for all the activities done on your site. This includes the comments your audiences leave and also the comments left by you.
  - Make it obvious to all your visitors that no abuse will be tolerated.
  - You should instantly clear off most of the annoying and offensive remarks.
  - If you find an individual giving negative or offensive remarks, then care them immediately.
  - If you want to state some private things to someone, don't use sites to achieve that.

Now, do you have the answer to what exactly is blogging? Those who know how to make full use of blogging discover it very intriguing. Additionally, blogs could be financially helpful for your company and business. On the flip side, you're going to get negative comments when you show your anger or frustration on your blog. Keeping your site clean and avoiding negative comments will allow you to construct a fantastic reputation. It will also create a positive opinion on people who read your blog.

Common Attributes of Blogs

Most online businesses today are highly reliant on SEO services for the promotion of their sites. Blogging is just one of the effective procedures for site promotion. So what is blogging? It is an act of creating a site an abbreviation of weblog'. This sort of site is maintained frequently, and it features diary-type posts and links to other articles or websites with associated contents. Most sites' contents have one specific topic in attention, like a healthy diet plan and sports. Others are more private that defines the person's reports about his ideas or comment on a piece of particular news, event, or movie.

Besides a few exceptions, most blogs have some things in common. One of which is your material, which is a collection of articles or posts which are usually arranged in chronological order with the latest on the top. The posts are usually organized into classes. The blog content ranges from private like observations and testimonials to news and politics. Some sites might have more than one author who writes their article or articles but all about precisely the same topic. Blog articles are usually composed at a web-based interface that's built into the blogging program. But we have what we called 'stand-alone weblog client applications' that let authors write posts offline and can be submitted later. The material is the most important characteristic of the site because the content is what blogging is.

Another thing found in most blogs is the comment box, where individuals can leave their comments regarding the post. This attribute makes the website an interactive one since viewers can express their beliefs about what the author writes, and subsequently, the writer can add his reply. There's also what we called 'pingbacks' or 'trackbacks' where authors of other blogs can leave a comment even without seeing the site. Other characteristics of a site are an archive of older articles based on dates such as monthly or annual archives, blog roll (the list of links to other related blogs or websites), and also one or more feeds such as RDF files and RSS.

Some blogs may possess other attributes besides what was cited. However, essentially, what is blogging is all about those basic features. Blogging is fun, but there are times when bloggers get put off due to a few people or no comments received. One has to have patience and must understand how to enhance his website to get success. For business functions, there are already lots of businesses that offer distinct search engine optimization services, which include blogging. These solutions are very useful for promoting online organization.

- **How to Decide What to Blog On**

Many people begin blogging to express themselves whether through random thoughts or as a method of keeping daily records of the lives or travels, by composing poetry or stories or simply by placing up their photos.

In most cases, what starts as a mish-mash of stuff slowly but surely begins to take shape. After making several posts, the site starts to have a distinct personality. It becomes a blog on a certain subject, subject, difficulty, motive, genre, or even of a specific kind of tone (say funny or amusing).

For many people, it has been very tough to decide ahead; what they are exactly likely to blog. What their blog's subject or tone and design is likely to be. All of this develops as the website grows.

This report provides all of the regular netizens and blogging newbie simple guidelines about how best to choose what to blog on. It will act like an easy guide about how to pick a blogging topic, subject, genre, or tone.

By sheer common belief, the Easiest Way to decide on which your site Topic ought to be is via elimination. Let us begin by removing one of two basic sorts of sites the personal blog and also the non-personal blog.

Very widely, blogs can be private or non-personal. Personal Blogs are on your personal thoughts, perspectives, artistic self-expression via artwork, music, poetry, videos, or anything else whatsoever of a private nature.

Non-personal blogs are based on anything that isn't personal. It may be on other people's views, thoughts, lives, artwork, songs, interests, etc., and may or may not have your additional views in them.

Let us take examples to describe this better. Suppose you start a blog in that you write on your experiences while traveling across the planet, it turns into a blog about you, and also what occurred to you. It turns into a personal site.

On the other hand, if you have a blog that's centered about the best movies being published in Hollywood, it turned into a non-personal website. Even if you state your views on such pictures, they are non-personal, because your primary subject isn't you, or whatever created or composed or foundation your own experiences or self-expression.

Well, let's now assume you have removed non-personal blogs. Now you're left with the arena of private blogs. Personal sites could be broadly and very rudimentarily broken up into three types: your experiences, any self-expression, or your individual views.

If you decide to eliminate self-expression and private views, you are left with experiences. Blogs on personal experiences could be of many types, but lets for the sake of simplicity shot these: Traveling experiences, daily adventures, Professional experiences, recreational adventures, spiritual adventures, dating experiences.

Suppose you zoom into recreational adventures; then, you've got a plethora of options - eating adventures, partying adventures, sports experiences, cinematic experiences, theatre experiences, and many others.

Let us assume that you choose to remove all except ingestion experiences. You have finally come down to blog on some very specific subject. You will blog on all the gastronomic adventures you have in the course of your own life. Be it ingestion in a vague restaurant in your home city, or having the neighborhood food of Hawaii or the special dinner your spouse cooked. You'll be writing on your adventures with meals, and that becomes the topic of your site.

Quite straightforward; however, there is a barrier to a significant number of choices. However, this hurdle becomes a boon, because you will never be able to identify all the options and may identify only some of these. The good thing about that is the fact that if you could not think of certain choices, it is because you are not even considering them. So they get automatically eliminated.

Likewise, if you'd removed private and preferred non-personal, you go about in an identical way to get rid of the options and achieve the most suitable one. As a basic example, we can say there are options like a star, engineering, finance, novels, character, etc. Using exactly the identical way as we did to the private blogs, along with your creativity and common sense, you'll have the ability to rapidly find out precisely what you wish to site.

- **How to Start A Wordpress Blog**

How to Design a Blog Logo in 5 Easy Steps
You've selected a current Market, place your Site or blog, and so are all set to put the final touches on your site until you go live and spread your information to the whole world.

Now the primary site designs are this manner; it's the right time to better off your site employing a cool logo!

Each Website and website takes a symbol, no matter if you are a little business blogger or even a hobbyist with lots of knowledge about a specific subject.

Don't get me wrong; your emblem is not just for your site. You'll also use it on your social media WebPages like Facebook, Twitter, Instagram, etc. to help spread the word about your website and brand.

Why Do You Need a Blog Logo?
For worse or better, you may find many million other bloggers around the world, and the chances are that anything you will likely write about was coated.

When People get into a Site for the very first time, they're very likely to desire a means to remember that you out of all the other websites on your specialty, along with your logo, is your visual indication that will aid them to achieve that.

Besides, owning a Web Site Logo can help you:

- Produce an excellent first impression. If made well, it will immediately pique the eye of your customers and encourage them to take a peek at your site.

- Position yourself as a strength by creating a logo that tells your viewers that your website is professional and that you're able to write about the subjects at hand.

- Build brand awareness. As a part of your own new, a logo can permit you to stand out on your specialization and construct awareness among your viewers.

- Make a new individuality. Your logo would be the base of your brand new, and it is going to permit you to make an emotional connection with your audience that turns them into loyal readers.

Kinds of Blog Logos
Generally, you may find nine types of Logos, which fall under three main categories: Icon-based, text-based, and blend marks (symbols which have both symbols and symbols).

For Websites, the most frequent type of Logo is a word-mark logo or a logo that is derived from the name of your website, whether the comprehensive title or a monogram nothing else. These trademarks put a good deal of focus on the typeface you are using. (We shall explore that in more detail below.)

Nonetheless, you might also go the mixture mark route and find a logo that conveys something related to a website name or the type of content you're likely to be submitting.

We'd recommend against an icon alone because it might be harder for audiences to join the emblem with your website if it doesn't have your name to follow it. Remember, your logo will have the ability to assist you in building brand recognition, which usually means you are likely to require a design your audience might easily remember.

Together with that said and done, allow us to reach the actual designing! Below are five steps that will assist you in producing the perfect blog logo.

- **5 Easy Steps to Designing a Blog Logo**

1. Think about your audience.

That is potentially the most important part of your entire emblem design process because it will notify the rest of the decisions you produce from the following steps.

Whether you're a lifestyle, personality, traveling, or private finance website, the logo you design needs to resonate with a specific audience, so for it to do the job required.

Contemplate your topic matter, and then consider that the ideal reader is best for this specific subject. Which kind of people will shortly be drawing to your website? Who are you hoping to reach? Try to compose some identifying details on your intended audience, for example, their assumed demographics and demographics.

How come this is significant? Well, a logo that uses thick fonts and lots of vivid colors wouldn't be acceptable for a website about depression, such as on the occasion you site about healthful living, a logo with a minimalist layout and dim because the essential color most likely won't appeal to your intended audience.

Make certain that you get an excellent notion of these folks that your website is assumed to entice before continuing to step 2.2. Choose a color palette.

The Colors you utilize in your emblem needs to be consistent with or complementary to this color scheme of your site or website.

In case you haven't yet chosen a motif to your website, each the energy for you, you can assemble your subject all-around your logo! But within this phase, many bloggers now have a website ready to sell, which generally contains a template (or even when you're using WordPress (a theme).

The most important thing to know is that the colors you choose will convey a particular set of feelings to your audiences. Each color has its own "character," and subsequently affects individuals to feel or feel about something unique. Employing example, red stimulates enthusiasm and energy, although blue is due to assurance, ability, and dependability. Do your homework color psychology before choosing your emblem color palette.

Additionally, you need to understand logo colour combinations that work well together and the ones that don't as well. Much like you want your logo colors to coordinate with your website, you should be certain they match each other both in appearance and in importance.

When choosing on your logo colors, opt to get a total of 2; a few more than that (cluttered design), and you are likely to distract your visitors from not getting a clear message.

Though it's the fact that electronic Mediums like blogs and websites are a bit more forgiving of vibrant symbols, in the event, you expect to brand offline also (such as using business cards or swag), then you'll require a symbol that looks as good in print as it does online.

3. Choose the perfect font.

If you have opted to pick a word-mark Emblem in your blog, then this step is the bread and butter on your logo. Your font will be the primary visual component than the goals of your audience, which usually means you'll want to choose one that best expresses the personality of your website and brand.

(Even if you've comprised an icon on your style, your font will still require a lot of weight, and thus don't skip this step).

There are four big sorts of fonts that are used in logos, even though website logos tend to favor script fonts and custom typefaces to present another amount of creativity into the design.

Nevertheless, exactly like with colors, the Ribbon (s) you use should be in contact with your web site audiences. Again, this relies upon the nature of the website; big, astonishing screen fonts, for example, wouldn't be suitable for a website on taxation data or accountancy. If you run a however gratifying travel website, boisterous decoration will almost certainly be the ideal move.

Additionally, be sure to take clarity into thought; some fonts, especially the "creative" ones that dominate site logos, can be challenging to browse, which defeats the goal of having a website logo.

Remember your website visitors will need to have the capability to read and understand the name of your website in the logo in a glance, therefore if it's a decision between a cool font alongside a plain but legible font, then proceed with the latter.

4. Produce a few variants.

Now, you have to have selected the individual elements of your design (like an icon in the event you're using one). Now, it's time to assess lots of iterations of your logo and pick that'll look best on your site.

You are going to want fun with colors of the specific same color palette or fonts at the specific same typeface household to guarantee each element works well together.

Additionally, produce a few different layouts and tweak the positions of each part. Is it true that the logo works better together with the center and text? Think about your icon for the best? Style five or four variations of your logo and decide which one best tells the story of your blog.

See that the dimensions of this Emblem positioning area differ from theme to theme, dependent on the website hosting system you're using. On some, the logo area will most likely be rather small, while on the others, it's often quite big. Irrespective of the dimensions, your logo needs to be transparent and simple to navigate; hence, before choosing a previous design, analyze your logo in unique dimensions to be sure the resolution looks terrific.

5. Choose the design process.

As soon as you experience an idea of how the Emblem will take shape, it's the right time to actually make it!

If you would like to go the DIY route, then you may use layout applications like Photoshop, offline or on-line emblem makers, or maybe attempt emblem manufacturer programs should you've got to look about the go.

- **Getting Your Blog Launched**

Blogging is becoming a favored instrument for communication info. There are a variety of programs for a site, such as delivering information on a specific subject matter, discussing experiences, and informative. Below is a quick overview of the actions involved with getting your website off the ground:

1. Choose on the subject or base of this website. You do not need to know everything about the topic you have chosen to site about as soon as you start. Frequently the best method to discover something is always to teach around it to other men and women. However, be sure you appreciate the topic, are excited about it, and have a great impulse to discuss your insights, inspiration, and wisdom with other people. Regularly adding content to your website will go a little while. And if you are enthusiastic about your subject, it's going to be a whole lot simpler to create and create ordinary posts.

2. Do your research. Before you choose a topic, do some researches on the internet to discover the number of websites that now exist on the topic? If you locate a whole lot of websites, which will notify you, there's already some curiosity about whatever you want to state. Doing this research will help identify the focus and will supply you with some amazing tips that you may incorporate into your site.

3. Receive a domain name. Whenever you have determined by a topic, you have got to get a domain from a registrar. It simply costs a little more than $10 a year for a domain. We suggest NameCheap because of their website's simplicity and simplicity of use, but various registrars sell domain names. While buying a domain name, it is best to get a domain name with a.com; nevertheless, .net and .org can also be normally utilized.

You'll find other rules to follow when creating your domain. Avoid using numbers and Roman numerals. Besides, you ought to try to obtain a domain without dashes breaking key words. There is some disagreement in the blogging community about this; however, you'd love to try and develop a domain name with no dashes. And steer clear of very long domain names - theyarehardforyourclientstoremember.com! And here is a hint: type out the word and determine if it creates any words which you don't have to view. Employing an example, we recently created a domain employing the phrases "crush it" in the name. When those two phrases have been squished together, it generates a 4-letter word! And that generated a few difficulties.

4. Host your domain name. You will need a WebHost. This costs around $10 per month. And On occasion, it is possible to discover a WebHost marginally cheaper. However, we advise you don't use a free blogging site like Blogspot.com or even WordPress.com. Why? Since you do not have complete control over what happens with your website. In the event you construct a website on those kinds of free blogging sites, you might eliminate all your job and effort when for whatever reason, your website is eliminated. And when it is not backed up, that may be a great deal of effort dropped, so do obtain a paid web host.

5. Create your website. When the Domain name is pointed to some WebHost, log in your website and set it into WordPress blogging software. This step is very involved, and above, we'll enter within this document. You may elect to pay for a website business to come across the fundamentals set up for you. In reality, there are hundreds and hundreds of WordPress themes accessible that change the overall look and texture of your website. And these themes can be

customized with your colors, banner, logo, and a great deal more! You can undoubtedly create a particular style for your site.

6. Install plug-ins. You are almost done with getting your website off the ground. As soon as the WordPress site software is set up, it's possible to put in plug-ins. The target of the plug-ins is to boost the program's functions beyond what the basic WordPress app does. For example, a plug-in may do automated backing out of your website, or display spam comments, or optimize your website content for search engines, and much more. And many Plug-ins are free.

7. Time to start blogging. When your site is prepared to go, it is the right the ideal time to begin entering site entrances. Consistency is vital. You'd love to give quality, constant blog entries to keep your audience engaged and thinking about whatever you want to convey. In the event you post linked, interesting content, you are going to receive traffic, you are going to get subscribers, and you're going to produce a neighborhood or later.

On a previous note, sites have a lot of platforms that they could be incorporated into, accomplishing a wider audience. They could be incorporated into websites, connected to social sites and article sites. And cross-linking your website using various platforms such as social networking websites raises traffic to each.

CHAPTER THREE
FREELANCE WRITING

Freelance writing now is a profitable business opportunity. As an online medium has come to be a significant source of info sharing, an increasing number of companies are moving online. It has increased the need for articles, and authors as any site designed for whatever motive should require some content within it. Additionally, to save cash and receive concentrations for their principal business, a lot of men and women outsource material composing, bringing a chance for freelance authors.

Numerous kinds of freelance writing will be innovative writing, eBook composing, sales and advertising writing, editorial and newsletter, magazine writing, SEO writing, website writing, and a lot more that we'll discuss in subsequent chapters.

The way to construct a successful freelance writing career

Even though for authors to break in the freelance marketplace, you will find lots of chances, but it demands correct and skilled strategy to accomplish success. Let us find out some brighter ways to achieve in various stages of your advertising career.

1. Start-up Phase

* Assess your abilities and interests: It is imperative to evaluate yourself before offering your solutions to the marketplace. Psychotherapy is adaptable, and you may select tasks that fit your attention, education, abilities, and history.

* Preliminary investigation: Actively hunt online for freelance jobs accessible and get yourself enrolled with assorted fantastic freelance writing websites online.

* Publish your solutions to prospects: A nicely designed "Bio-sheet', is a very best source to provide to the potential customer. It's a

document very similar to your resume carrying out a short outline of your education, abilities, interests, and experiences.

2. Growing Phase

* Beware of this single-client snare: As freelancer work is a project established and normally no contracts have been signed, it's essential to work for several customers instead of adhering to one customer, but you need to avoid giving solutions to customers who may be others near competitors.

* Enhance your writing skills: To be able to sustain your tasks, it's essential to maintain improving your writing abilities. In later chapters, we'll discuss in detail how exactly do you enhance your writing abilities and be consistent.

* Require criticism positively: Require opinions and criticism from your customers as recommendations for future achievement rather than get frustrated on rejections.

3. Maturity Stage

* Be persistent: Consistency is vital for long-term existence. It's generally discovered that outsourcing is thought of as a source of instant income, and people consider it quite lightly and have bored too fast.

* Stay connected with older customers: Link building is regarded as a secret to success because the marketplace is saturated with masses of most freelance authors from throughout the world.

- **Six Tips For A Powerful Freelance Writing Career**

Organization and time management are a freelance author's best buddies. Freelance authors that are fresh for the culture will love liberty and liberty. Instead of simply cubicle walls, freelancers may operate on the outside, a Starbucks, library, or perhaps the shore. Nevertheless, behind this lifestyle demands discipline not as operating from the business world. Although you chucked that lawsuit for collapses, you might be fighting with growth and finding it hard to carry on more missions. From the freelance writing arena, the quicker you can finish a mission, the more income you may make. Try out these suggestions to create a more successful freelance writing profession:

1) Maintain a daily laptop, especially for your freelance writing function, which might feel strange at first, particularly in an era where data can be saved electronically, but various studies have proven the finger and hand motions of composing the regions in the mind that participate in thinking, language, and memory. Write the date at the top of a webpage in list and notebook out jobs or "to-do's" in bullet points. Check off each activity as it's completed. Add new missions or tasks for this list during the day. The following afternoon, date a brand new page, compose the "to-do's" left out of the day before, and then repeat the procedure.

Two) Organize your house office workspace by removing jumble of scratch paper and sticky notes. Hang a whiteboard on the walls and then write on it your present and forthcoming freelance writing assignments or job and your deadlines, and also utilize your everyday notebook to write anything generally boils down to a sticky note. A laptop with tabs works nicely for all those freelance authors who want to divide their own everyday "to-do" record from notes on the study, customer talks and appointments, and other freelance writing tasks.

3) Keep track of the time daily working as an independent author, if your actions involve advertising your abilities, corresponding with customers or real writing. Be aware of the true period of the day that you began and finished work. This looks counter to the rule of liberty within freelance writing; however, it's vital to view how much of this day is spent working, as you are the sole employee — tracking of work hours aids in gauging time spent on a mission. If you're spending additional time on a job than initially expected, this is a notification of project or customer and can assist in calculating the hourly rate for comparable writing jobs or in ascertaining whether to take missions from this customer later on.

4) Function depending on your natural mental condition. Some freelance authors tend to be more mentally awake in the daytime and operate from the steam in the day, while some are hard-working by their next cup of morning java and then hit their stride at the day. The very best time to compose or perform jobs that need mental attention or critical thinking is if you're mentally alert. More regular activities like reading emails, bidding on jobs, exploring, and invoicing should be performed if you find it hard to devote your focus on filling the display before you with persuasive, smart words.

5) Strategize to work as you work. Utilize the time following that you "clock out" as a freelancer Author for private activities. When blending work with paying home debts, walking the dog, going grocery shopping, or other private errands, it's more challenging to evaluate how long is really spent on freelance writing projects. Additionally, once you congregate work in 3-4 hour blocks, you are normally a lot more effective than when needing to find out where you left off many times for the day.

6) Get out of these pajamas and slippers and Get dressed. It is very important to find yourself as no more different than your counterparts operating on cubicles under artificial lighting. It does not necessarily need to mean placing a tie or sporting heels, but keeping the ritual of dressing up for a job can help to promote an awareness of worth and self-respect to the freelance writing career.

7) Switch off the television and application the DVR. Television only creates another diversion for the mind to need to sort out to focus on the job at hand. For freelance writers that enjoy having audio of the TV in the background while they operate, look at playing audio on speakers instead of picking up that distance.

8) Get out of the house. If you don't possess another office in a house in which you can shut the doorway from out, non-freelance composing diversions, consider working a couple of hours beyond the home. Do a bit of research and check the various Starbucks, Peets, or alternative regional coffeehouses to ascertain which ones offer the very best working environment for you. Besides comfort and convenience, start looking for Wi-Fi accessibility, client density, and sound levels throughout the hours you will be there working out.

For your freelance author, time does interpret into money. The more efficient utilization of your time along with also the more organized your home office is, the more efficient you are, so a larger earning potential and far better achievement to the freelance writing career.

- **How to Start a Freelance Website**

Step-by-Step Guide: How to Produce a Successful Freelance Site
We are all aware that an active existence on the World Wide Web is essential for any business enterprise. But for salespeople that do not necessarily provide their creative thoughts on a stand-alone or function from a mortar and brick, an internet presence is an absolute necessity. The quantity of jobs that freelancers got online has considerably improved over the past years -- no matter the specialization. This is possibly true for you, too. Chances are you already have societal reports or a committed page exhibited through internet directories, and this is excellent. But you ought to be aware that it's just insufficient. What makes the distinction between a normal company and a success story is a whole, client-catching site.

As you already possess some technical abilities plus a natural talent to do things yourself, making your freelancer site is a clear alternative. Not only does it save money but also the bother of needing to utilize an outside business. With the ideal set of resources, it is possible to shatter any imaginative border and construct a gorgeous online portfolio by yourself.

Thus, to generate life easier for you, we have compiled a comprehensive step-by-step manual that's guaranteed to take your company to another level. Here are the actions that you have to have to make an independent site for your business enterprise.

01. Choose a design
Much like you would not begin driving before entering the address of the destination into your GPS then, you ought to think of what exactly the perfect design (the visual arrangement of your website) is before beginning to work with it. Ask yourself these questions: which components do you wish to stand outside? What's the first/last thing people see when they go entered? How can you imagine the circulation of your website?

You can begin from a blank canvas or select one of the stunning templates offered for creative individuals' use. It is possible to choose if you would like to utilize these templates to get pure inspiration or provide them an extreme makeover, then which makes them even to the men and women who made them. On the opposing side of this spectrum, beginning your site from scratch will let you go complete experimental and build from the ground up. If you are still looking for inspiration, then why don't you look at these several sites of specialists which you respect and see how they've organized their job?

02. Brand it directly
Your site is exactly like a newborn infant. To begin with, you have to give it a title. Produce a couple of unique alternatives and assess which ones have an accessible (and fitting) domain. Next, you will need to think about SEO. Folks have to have the ability to find you via search engines such as Google. Ideally, your domain name must include the title of your biz along with also a flavor of everything you do -- such as www.johnsmith-video.com. This guide is going to allow you to find the ideal domain name for the enterprise.

After planting a domain name, then it is time to include your visual speech. Significantly, it stands outside, however in precisely the same time contrasts with the remainder of your advertising, either online (social stations, campaigns, advertisements, etc.) and offline (brochures, decals, business cards, etc.). This applies to an emblem, your fonts, and your color palette along with your variety of pictures. Each of the components of your company should talk with a single voice and a single voice just.

03. Insert the applicable pages
Now it is time to split out the cake. Consider all of the articles that you would like to disperse across your site and strategically pick the ideal method to arrange it based on your objectives. You also can add as many pages (or segments) for a website; however, these would be the most crucial you need to add:

· Homepage: Consider this as the entry to your site. Here is the very first thing website visitors will strike. Do not neglect to incorporate some descriptive text. Many designers presume that a gorgeous background picture will do all of the talking. When in actuality, it is a mistake. Clients will need to understand who you are fully and everything you do and that they will need to understand it immediately once they enter your website. Additionally, the text is vital to your Google rank. Choose your words wisely and ensure every piece of text will be to the stage, and each photograph or movie is the ideal match to procure a terrific first impression.

· Services: Produce a very clear and thorough section describing what sort of goods or services that you offer. Choose whether you want to enable clients to place requests or orders by your website, and comprise CTAs (requires for actions) to encourage them to achieve that.

· Jobs: Emphasize your character and high quality of work by embracing chosen projects and also a listing of respected customers who've selected to work together with you. Pick your beautiful and up-to-date creations (that the Wix Guru Gallery is a fantastic way to display them).

· Guarantee: To be able to exploit the ability of satisfied clients, include a testimonial segment, or perhaps a complete page. Client reviews possess the highest potency score for articles advertising at 89 percent. Allow real folks to talk about their positive experiences concerning you.

· About webpage: Use this site to show your business' strengths and provide essential information regarding your actions and outline your distinctive individuality, work ethic, and values.

· Contact: Once you have stunned them along with your website, visitors need to be able to contact you easily. Insert a touch' type, your email, telephone numbers, social websites, along with another approach to achieve you. Additionally, adding your information at the Footer of your site is regarded as a great practice.

Extras (but highly recommended):
· FAQ: This webpage may contain the most requested questions that individuals may produce. Utilize an FAQ site to conserve time by offering responses to repeating queries, sweep off clients' concerns, and boost your website's visibility on Google.

· Website: By always publishing and creating new content, your site can help enhance your search engine optimization rank, in addition to establishing yourself as a professional in your area. Uncertain how to begin?

Online shop: It is time to earn some cash! Sell digital copies of your job directly from your site using Wix Art Store, a fresh and 100 percent commission-free alternative for photographers, artists, and designers.

04. Make it glow using sophisticated design attributes
Your Site is much more than only a method to an end. It is also an additional outlet that you express your talent and imagination, and reveal that you are together with your visual match. Create a listing of all of the trendy design qualities you think will enhance your articles and get started researching which ones are going to have the ability to easily be incorporated to your website. Caution: you do not need to spoil it. Carefully and add just what functions. Some cases

include hover impacts, customized grids, parallax scrolling, and animation. For every result, consider just how it should look to some first-time guests and think about the purpose it ought to function. The fantastic thing is you don't require any programming knowledge to attain at least one of these outcomes. We have obtained some outstanding layout characteristics which are already installed, waiting for you to work with and customize them.

05. Locate the ideal business tools

As a freelancer, then you are accustomed to performing things yourself. But occasionally (like anyone), you might also use a little bit of additional assistance. Your site can readily be converted into a quick, dependable personal helper. Besides a range of visual strengths and attributes for your website, Wix provides a useful set of tools to help simplify the management of particular facets of your business enterprise. Like every business operator, communicating with your customers is an integral part of your everyday routine. No less significant is the prospective clients' ability to conduct business with you via an automatic internet system. Fortunately, you can enable clients to schedule appointments (or courses) using an internet booking/payment platform such as Wix Bookings. It's possible to make online reservations 24/7, take secure obligations, send automated mail reminders, and much more.

06. Prove your technician abilities

Prove your layout and creative abilities by showing your customers that you can create complex web applications. Corvid from Wix permits you to fit all of the code components which you would like to make for your site, for more comfortable and more specialist software. By way of instance, if you are a graphic designer, you may use it to execute your designs inside the various custom made connections. By doing this, you are going to create your site more participating and concurrently promote your services. Make the most of this effective tool by gathering vital information regarding your clients' tastes through lively pages by producing forms and inspection segments. Corvid offers innovative code capacities and a user interface, which makes it incredibly quick to grasp the very best part. Corvid works flawlessly with the magnificent visual elements of this Wix. The editor also can be completely SEO compatible.

07. Do your Search Engine Optimization homework
What's an Internet presence if nobody gets to view it? This is precisely the reason you need to spend a little time and effort into your SEO (search engine optimization). For your customers to quickly find you and also reserve your solutions, you have to be certain that your site appears in a fantastic position in search results (such as Google). Search engine optimization is a continuous undertaking of a variety of elements of your website. We have the best manual for all about SEO. You will learn, as an instance that you will need to keep your content fresh and your information updated. Writing a website is one method of accomplishing precisely that, but besides, it applies to some other kind of written articles on your site. Keywords are also a vital element. You will need to be certain you locate the proper keywords of people, the words which the majority of people would type into Google when searching for a company similar to yours. When you've completed some keyword research, you are going to use these small gems in strategic areas through your site.

Some salespeople occur to have a permanent place, or an area of action (think about a wedding photographer who operates in a particular town). This is the area where neighborhood search engine optimization comes in to play. The principal goal here would be to ensure your site is seen by anyone looking in your distinct place. Neighborhood SEO best practices include: maintaining your company on Google My Business, registering your site on important directories, and incorporating your place on your site's pages.

Extra suggestion: Should you've got a Wix site, try out the Wix SEO Wiz. It is a step-by-step plan intended to help improve your website's SEO using a tailored checklist and useful tips.

08. Believe mobile-friendly
Often, when Folks are designing a site, they overlook that a (huge) number of consumers will most likely be seeing their website out of a Smartphone. Just as a matter of fact, 75 percent of consumers may access the Web from cellular devices in 2018. Therefore, among the more important challenges salespeople have to confront in regards to their internet presence is assuring, it will be compatible with phones. Thinking about the little display, you are going to want to reinstall

the cell version of your website, keeping just the most vital elements observable. What's more, look closely at the fonts and colors that you use and make sure they are readable. Lower the total amount of typing needed and think about including a research bar to facilitate navigation. If you are a blessed Wix user that your website will automatically create a mobile-friendly edition, using a flexible gallery to your images.

09. Assess and discuss
Last, however, listen to exactly what a near friends have to say regarding the content along with the visuals you picked on your website. Let them know it is a secure space and request constructive criticism. Believe it is far better to listen to it out of close friends as opposed to your "buddies" on social networking. When you have printed your website, do not neglect to discuss it on all your social stations. You will reach more prospective clients, enhance your search engine optimization ranking, and discover frank opinions on your most recent creation. Besides, by incorporating societal buttons to your website, visitors will have the ability to attain your social networking profiles readily.

When you've obtained the word out, keep in mind that running a successful site is not a 100-meter sprint but instead a marathon. There is another tweak to be forced to make it somewhat better. Keep upgrading your articles, implement new features, enhance your user experience, and remain current with current design trends. Oh, and brace yourself, since the company offers are just about to come pouring in.

- **10 Steps The Way to Begin a Freelancing Business While Working Full-Time in 2020 (and Why You Should)**

With more than 54 million Americans preferring to forego conventional professions and begin an independent company which gives them greater flexibility to make a lifestyle that they love, we see an unprecedented change in how businesses work around the globe.

Hiring Managers has become not just more suitable but more appealing to many companies. This produces an amazing chance for those who have useful abilities to begin an outsourcing company across the other side, and finally develop that to some sustainable self-improvement livelihood. Exactly, that is what I've achieved with my content promoting adviser enterprise.

Fewer taxation, lower employee-related expenditures, no health care, much less office space, the list continues. All these are but a small number of reasons many organizations are looking for freelancer authors, designers, and programmers to help expand their companies. And for freelancers, you will find many good freelance jobs sites cropping up; fulfill this need now, the chances are just getting better and better.

A recent analysis at the University of Phoenix, polling 1,600 adults under the age of 30, found that 63 percent of men and women in their 20's own their own company or wish to in the not too distant future. Of those that aren't currently entrepreneurs, 55% recognized as needing to be one day.

So, how do those people, irrespective of age, want to be gainfully self-conscious head about getting started using our professions as entrepreneurs? Well, opting to initiate an independent company is among the most viable, realistic, and achievable side of companies possible to begin while maintaining your day job (along with the safety that comes with this).

1. Establish Your Goals
Without clearly defined, readily quantifiable objectives, you are likely to have an extremely hard time getting into where you would like to go.

Is freelance a route to only getting extra cash on both sides of the daily job?
Can you finally wish to turn into a full-time freelancer due to the lifestyle advantages of becoming your boss?
Or, why are you wishing to utilize outsourcing as a stepping stone to finally achieving another target entirely?

Whatever your ultimate aim is, you have to make it abundantly apparent. Here is something which each one the planet's top entrepreneurs agree on when it regards successfully launching a company.

Take the time to understand why you are thinking about beginning an independent firm --do you wish to become an independent author, Freelance designer, or Freelance programmer? Ensure this choice is the ideal move on your development toward attaining your larger image objectives.

Just after you've got the clarity about where you need Freelancing to carry you, will you get started financing into your shorter-term targets and benchmarks that will assist your freelance business to become a hit.

On the Millo site, April Greer shares among my favored requirements on the significance goal-setting inside your freelance company, and the way to establish meaningful targets that move you ahead.

Let us say your larger image goal is to eventually become a fully Self-evident freelancer. You will set your hours, choose which you need to utilize, and call most of the shots in your company. But how can you arrive?

You know that you will need to get your freelance earnings upward into a sustainable, healthful degree, which lets you eventually quit your daily life without worry about where your next paycheck will come out of. Because I have stopped my day job also premature previously together with the telephone case company I began (and ended up going in with my buddy for a couple of months), my rule is that I must accomplish a negative income of 75% of what my entire job pays me, until considering quitting to pursue my own unwanted company full-time.

Beginning with your freelance revenue goal, according to your living expenditures, risk tolerance, along with realistic expectations regarding how long your savings may sustain you, you can now back into a general idea of the number of clients you will need (and what you are going to have to bill them), before making it to this point at which you are going to have the ability to leave your day job to freelance full-time.

2. Locate a Profitable Niche

Let us assume you are a graphic designer by trade, or you have been constructing your abilities with Adobe Illustrator & Photoshop in your spare time.

Certainly, there will be a good deal of competitors in your industry that will be eager to charge substantially lower prices than you, regardless of what you're doing. There are people from all over the globe with reduced costs of living that will remain inclined to take lesser-paid gigs than you personally. Get over the notion of attempting to compete on cost for a freelancer, correct today.

It is not worth hurrying different folks to the base for function from home occupations on an independent basis, particularly if websites such as Fiverr, Upwork, or alternative freelance jobs websites have countless alternatives for low-cost freelancers. Side note: I recommend never list your solutions on both of those websites if you don't have to (after striking from trying all within this article first).

By choosing the time to discover a lucrative market for your Freelance business (as you would select a market to site about if you decide to start a website), you are actively searching for a business and sort of customer that appreciates quality. When you are in an area that competes on quality, then you will completely alter the manners where you market your solutions. You are going to be competing for value, not cost.

Rather than carrying any graphic design job that includes your way, opt to concentrate exclusively on infographic style for startup sites, or eBook designs for technology businesses. Pick a place that interests you and also concentrate on getting the very best designer in that narrow area; that is the way you locate the ideal side hustle market. When you've assembled your abilities to a degree which you may confidently charge a premium for, and then you are prepared to begin your freelance company and search for your perfect customers.

As soon as you've made yourself valuable in your niche, you'll have a stage by which you'll be able to enlarge your freelance company in almost any way you would like later on. As opposed to stressing about the way you are likely to get in step 0 to 100, consider freelancing one little step at one time. Progress begets more advanced with your negative hustle.

3. Identify Your Target Customers
As significant as finding a lucrative market is bringing the ideal kinds of customers to your Freelance enterprise.

As you are just starting your freelance company, it is nice to bring a little more of a shotgun method of landing a few customers. Produce some initial assumptions about which you wish to utilize, aim them, and after dealing with a couple of these, you are going to create a very clear awareness of whether you need to keep on pursuing similar customers.

Since beginning my freelance business, I have honed my target customer profile over the years to fit just two very particular kinds of companies: high-growth technology startups and business influencers with well-established private brands.

The main reason I have narrowed down the attention of My Freelancer Company this way is since I operate best these kinds of (quite similar) customers, and they run into similar circles that cause regular referrals. I am building my standing within my market.

This is a Tricky choice to make initially, as it means turning off a great deal of company. On the other hand, the procedure for putting in your intended customers, which you work with, can allow you to achieve far greater outcomes in the long term. As soon as you've got a couple of customers that are eager to recommend for you, the endings are going to pick up. This is something Caroline Beaton has experienced lots of success together with if she has started together with her business.

Moving back to our attention on competing for value, not cost, all that you do concerning beginning your freelance business, particularly once you've got an extremely limited number of free time, need to return to your capacity to supply the highest quality outcomes for your clientele.

Your objective is to build your ability and finally be viewed as the go-to source for a particular kind of customer (s).

By enticing so nicely to some slim (well-selected) Market, your goal customers will have an extremely speedy route to determining that you are the ideal person to assist them with their jobs. This, above all else, is always your road to charging high rates without anybody batting an eye in the very first costs you throw away.

To ascertain the best type of goal customers as you get to begin an independent company, ask yourself the following three questions:

Which companies will locate my solutions usefully?
Which companies can pay the costs I will have to charge to reach my income target?
Who will be the decision-makers within those companies, and what do I learn about their demographics & pursuits? Could I find a means to join with them on an individual level?
Whenever you've got all this advice, you are going to be pleased to craft a chilly email that cuts right to the heart of these customers' needs; you will have the ability to join together and provide an instant price.
Together with my goal customers, smaller startup teams along with founders with private brands, they could immediately relate to me due to my inclination to startups and also certainly will select up with my fashion of content promoting strategy. Since my portfolio function is directly related to what they perform, they also begin with considerably more assurance that I will have the ability to induce similar outcomes to their small business, too.

4. Establish Strategic Costs on Your Services
I have spoken a great deal about establishing the ideal deals for your Freelancer Company before you begin. I architected an infographic that walks you through the practice of placing your freelancer hourly fee.

From a pure statistics standpoint, this freelancer rate explorer of Bonsai is equally as good as it makes for discovering what your expected hourly fee must exactly be for your business to be able to find out whether your prices will fulfill your income targets and cost levels. You will find a lot of great tools available for double-checking, which you are charging enough to pay for the lifestyle that you would like to dwell on, but I advise beginning to ascertain your pricing plan with a rather different development in your mind.

Bear in mind that you have to cost yourself according to the value you send, not depending on which your competitors are charging.

Do not let anyone dictate the terms in which you establish your worth. That is not exactly what beginning an outsourcing company is all about.

Digital marketing adviser Neil Patel chronicles a lot of the lessons that he learned while conducting a freelance Search Engine Optimization company on his website before he learned the way to earn money blogging in more passive ways. Among the most obvious classes that stuck to me personally, is the longer you bill, the fewer customers whine. Since he astutely has chosen target customers that have large budgets, so he understands they're considerably more prepared to shell out money to be able to earn back that money through investing in your providers.

Smaller customers, on the other hand, often don't possess as Much cash to play, and consequently cannot sustain much concerning losses when jobs do not deliver huge returns.

There is nothing as costs that are too significant. Your costs may be too large (or too low) to the kinds of customers you are targeting, but if you do your assignments into determining what to pitch your solutions to, then you are going to be promoting what your customers exactly need to get a cost they could justify.

In my freelance business, I compose well-researched, comprehensive Blog article thoughts for my customers (like I print here, that has been one of my initial motivations to find out the way to begin a blog at first position).

The majorities of my articles are in the assortment of 1,500 - 2,500 words Per bit and made to rank well in search results, which is very beneficial for many companies. Since my job goes beyond simply writing, and to strategic supply and driving visitors following the material releases, I add much more value for the customers than another "author" can bring to the table. For that excess price, my costs begin at $500 per article (plus supply) and harshly move up out there, according to additional prerequisites and add-ons.

Do not charge too much over your worth, but do not ever undervalue what you are doing for the clientele.

They are likely to employ someone to assist with their projects; therefore, it is only a matter of showing them you are the ideal person to assist. Cost becomes a secondary concern, even if they are already convinced that you are the ideal man for your job. It is a company, and they will make it function, also it was not intended to be.

Remember that you will not be the best person for each customer and that by simply displaying that you understand all of the company's presence and business jargon inside your market is not an indication of authority.

5. Construct a High-Quality Portfolio Website
Because I am such a massive advocate of creating a strong online existence to help beginning an independent company, I earned a professional, Laurence Bradford, to discuss each one of the vital components to constructing a freelancer portfolio that provides you, high-value customers. Here too, is my final guidance regarding the best way to begin a site (and generate income from it).

As a beginning point, let us know what the intent behind possessing a portfolio site is also in the first location. It is often the first impression a prospective customer will possess you, your personality, your job, and also the previous customers (or businesses) you have worked with on your freelance business. You have to effectively convey the services that you provide and that they are for. Beyond this, you have to market yourself on why you are the ideal person for this kind of job - to the customers that you would like to utilize.

Your freelancer portfolio wants to perform the next, to become truly capable of promoting your solutions:

Stress your area of specialization & screen examples of your job.
Organize your contact info & showcase your character.
Emphasize your relevant skills, education, and achievements.
Display reviews (even when they are out of colleagues or former supervisors when you are only getting started).
Have routine updates that show your development, new customers, and upgraded sample function.
As you are creating your portfolio Website, locate other Freelancers inside your area and find some inspiration from these to help discover how they are positioning themselves, inventing their worth propositions, and moving about building their companies.

6. Produce Examples of Things You May Deliver (in Your Portfolio Website)
You want your website to function as a destination to demonstrate your experience.

With that in mind, among the finest ways to demonstrate you are in the understanding side of your area is by frequently publishing new articles, pictures, or videos (determined by the material moderate you work in) that will amaze your target customers. As soon as you've got an understanding of exactly what your customers want, go outside and produce illustrations of the specific kind of content - like you'd been hired to create it for your site.

There is no greater way to market your providers than to show your customers that you're able to make what they require. What is more, is the fact that it will create their jobs that much simpler when you've got a library of associated work to pull out for inspiration.

My site is a living example of that. When I put out to begin an independent organization, I determined early on this at least one time a month, so I was planning to make it a point to print an extremely comprehensive 4,000+ phrase blog article on subjects that fall below instructing my subscribers how to begin and develop a lucrative side business, the subject of what on my website and something that I have intimate encounter with.

It is not denied that I choose to use customers who have a virtually identical goal market, as people who I talk to my private website here. All of my prospective customers will need to perform, is take a look at some of my articles to view how much involvement that they receive, pick up in my dialogue fashion, and get a sense of how I would have the ability to work together & their viewers.

If you are a web designer, then your portfolio website ought to be very thoroughly curated because everything concerning it is still a representation of that which you will have the ability to construct for your clientele. If you are a writer like me, then your site posts will need to consult with the caliber of work you will make for everybody you use. As an example, the same thing goes to make sure that the pictures you feature on your website are representative of this design that you would like to make for your prospective customers.

7. Thoughtfully Choose Your Initial Customers
Since you've got a very restricted quantity of time to supply new customers (and do the job for them) since you begin your freelance business, you want to get the absolute most from the customers you do attract on - the two from a fiscal and portfolio-building perspective.

Your restricted number of customers and correlating portfolio Bits will signify how you are perceived with other possible customers moving ahead.

This makes everybody you decide to utilize or emphasize on your site a vital choice - particularly initially. You do not need to overthink it goes into choice paralysis; however, spend a moment or two thinking through whether each possible client you are contemplating can enable you to reach where you would like to go.

Bonus points, if you are extremely orderly about monitoring your freelancer customers, leads with a tool like among my selections to your finest CRMs for a small company (and salespeople).

8. Mention Potential Clients on Your Content

Scouring the Web for your finest remote jobs will not necessarily net you immediate results. And you are likely to have difficulty creating a name for yourself in your specialty if no one knows you exist.

That is why in each piece of content that I produce in my Blog, I often mention the brands, businesses, and people I see myself possibly working with a single day. Even if I am not ready to undertake new customers, or I am not qualified to go after such enormous deals; nonetheless, it is never too early to begin establishing goodwill and getting your name in the front of the ideal people in your target businesses.

Do look forward to the information you intend creating to your Site within the forthcoming weeks, also maintain a running record of those firms that you need to incorporate if possible. Then, as soon as you release something, which mentions them take a couple of minutes to get out and then inform them about it.

I cannot emphasize enough how essential this step was in assisting me in beginning an independent company and developing my private brand so fast.

Nearly every time I do so, the individual I emailed reacts very fast with thanks, they will typically discuss it via their business social stations, plus they won't overlook it.

The majority of the time, you'll be top with a chilly Email to a person you have never talked to, yet this pushes out your comfort zone to remain healthy.

Here are the vital components of a purposeful cold Email, and here's my private template.

Explore the very best point of contact to get out to.
Always perfect on your topic line for your receiver.

Maintain your request brief.
Boost your strengths.
Always add a call-to-action.

9. Find out to reduce yourself

If you would like to begin freelancing, you have to understand the way to pitch yourself; it is an advantage that will be well worth its weight in gold for a long time to come.

No matter how proficient you're in your craft, if you would like to turn your abilities into starting an independent company, you have to have the ability to convey those advantages and convert your discussions into paying customers.

My whole (currently closed) class on Winning Freelance Customers Is devoted to the subject of how to locate, convince, and also convert new customers for your freelance company using carefully strategized suggestions and reach out strategies. And in addition to this, we discuss somewhat the way to drive visitors to your site, which stands a possibility of converting paying customers.

Here are the fundamentals of crafting a successful freelancer suggestion that lands your customers:

Create a solid entry with an elevator pitch email that currently provides immense price & shows you have completed your homework.
Boost your strengths.
Expect and answer some questions which may develop.
Lean on relevant work samples and previous endeavors to show your experience.
Utilize a visually attractive design for your proposition

10. Do Not Mix Your Day Job Priorities with Freelance Business

Above all, it is important to not forget that your day job (and only source of dependable income) is the number one priority.

Do not do anything to sabotage your full-time occupation, as you need it to keep you as you develop your freelance business on the other side. My comprehensive article on the best way to prevent getting fired (and sued) when starting a side business is worth reading since you begin with your freelance career.

There are whole lots of no-no's you will need to prevent, such as:

Breaching any contracts or arrangements you have signed with your employer.
Working on your freelance company during a business time (badly do NOT do so).
Utilizing business tools, computers, or compensated for blogging resources inside your freelance endeavors.

Now that you have obtained comprehension of how to begin a Freelance company, here is why I think everyone (particularly millennial) ought to be freelancing on the other side. It has been among the very best business decisions I have ever created, and it has been, by far, my most constant side industry to-date.

I strongly recommend anyone contemplating beginning a freelance company, or transitioning into being a consultant, start with Freelancing on the negative while still functioning full-time.

This is why.

- **Should You Start a Freelance Business While Working Full-Time?**

1. Assessing Out Self-Employment Stress-Free
You have to build up a runway of customers and income move until you up and stop your work unless you are prepared to discount potentially a lot of economies or take out a credit line to prop up yourself as you are not earning much cash with your freelance company or startup.

I am all for calculated risks, therefore that one is easy for me: I want to earn as much cash as my existing occupation affords me personally, or near to it (my principle is my side company should generate 75 percent of what my full-time pays me), so I can justify stopping to concentrate full-time on customer acquisition, even before I even think about departing.

By paying 10-20hrs/wk landing freelancer customers and working in their jobs, you are likely to receive a very clear estimate of how much work it's conducting your enterprise. Bookmark those inspirational quotations, since you may need them

Most of all, you'll be optimizing all your company practices without the strain of having the earnings since you still have your day task for it.

I am very lucky I adored the job I did in my day (Creative Live) once I began freelancing. It was purposeful, and daily I left excellent connections and built my brand while simultaneously driving exceptional results running the advertising for the company courses there. I was not in a situation where I wanted or wanted to leave my job up there so that I had the advantage of having the ability to begin my freelance company on the side with no strain of being in work, which was not fulfilling.

2. Growing Your Earnings
Among the greatest benefits of analyzing your way into starting an independent business as you're working full-time, is the extra income.

When it's a couple of hundred bucks, or a few million, you must keep careful track of all you are making through your freelancer side enterprise. I suggest using a lightweight CRM instrument such as Close or Sales flare, equally CRM methods for tracking your clientele and monitoring the progress you are making on prices, besides keeping tabs to the worth of every contract you are working on.

As you're steadily racking up your freelance earnings and signing more customers, I suggest saving 100 percent of your earnings from the freelancer enterprise. Before you get started, make certain to prepare a new checking account because of your destination for becoming compensated by freelance customers. This is very important for many reasons. You're going to be very definitely monitoring how much annual income your freelance business creates, it's going be in another account which you are unable to withdraw, and you are actively building a security net for possible lean days ahead.

3. Building Your Partner
Arguably the most important motive to start a freelancer Company as you're still functioning, you are likely to be receiving a great deal of expertise very quickly, you will be detecting your strengths and bettering your abilities under conditions which are in your hands. You are not under the gun to instantly take on millions of customers. Alternatively, you can concentrate on delivering very large-excellent work on a few projects which will enable you to continue to improve in your livelihood.

As a writer, I understand the importance of keeping up with tendencies and frequently practicing my skills. Whether I am writing to my site or for an independent client job, I have to experience the exercises that I wish to continue to improve on daily.

By minding my solutions, I am getting paid by others to boost my abilities.

And in the lead till all this, I exactly learned what a site is and educated myself a much more precious art set simply by going through the procedure of studying how to generate a site, picking from one of the best site builders, and publishing my writing online. That was the largest triumph.

While researchers haven't agreed on a set variety of hours, Clinic needed to eventually become an expert in any topic. The longer you spent maximizing your skills and creating your style, the greater. Recent research in Princeton revealed that the quantity of deliberate exercise one has might not correlate closely together with functionality, as formerly believed. Nonetheless, you'll experience immense advantages from working on your favorite abilities.

By Michael Jordan, on Bill Gates, they became exceptional at what they're doing, not because they place in an extraordinary time in practice, but since they cared profoundly about enhancing their skills and being the ideal.

Start practicing as quickly as you can so you will be able to control higher prices to my freelance company in the future.

4. Nailing Down Your Pricing Plan

When you initially begin an Independent Company, most people today tend to greatly undervalue their solutions and place the bar quite low at the start. This can be justified by attempting to establish rates based on "market value" or similar to other people in the business. This is completely backward, as you will need to be pricing your solutions dependent on the value you supply. However, many salespeople need to understand this lesson the hard way.

When you are bidding on a freelance job, always begin greater than you feel you need to. Concentrate on communicating just how much value you are likely to provide for the customer, and also lean heavily on results & accomplishments you have already created for different customers, or in your work.

Along with undervaluing your providers, it is simple to significantly underestimate the prices that go into conducting your freelance business. $35/hr in your 9-5 job is not the same as charging 35/hr to your services.

Now that you will soon be self-explanatory, it is time to familiarize yourself with each of the new taxation, fees, costs, and expenses of living that will soon be set on your shoulders that your employer may no longer be subsidizing some of these prices.

5. Making Your Brand

I am a firm believer that you are creating a personal new brand for yourself in all that you do. Deciding to begin an independent company and tie your title into the job you do to get a wide assortment of customers, is among the very best methods to begin getting your name into your industry.

How can you want the entire world to view you? In beginning a freelancing company, you'll come up with an internet portfolio to exhibit your functions and show off everything you could do for prospective customers.

You will need to make job proposition templates, sample functions, and pricing guides until you venture out and begin fostering customers. What better time have you to start creating these substances than while you still have a stable income from the day job?

CHAPTER FOUR
AFFILIATE ADVERTISING

For those who have ever contemplated trying to make money online, you likely did not need to look far to observe all sorts of merchandise and sites about Affiliate Marketing. Online affiliate marketing is one of the most frequent methods for ordinary people to make an income online. Since you might already understand, an affiliate is an internet-based agent for somebody else's merchandise. The majority of the e-books and internet marketing courses you've noticed online were likely advertised through an affiliate marketer, so if you understood it or not, you've been involved in affiliate marketing, except you're the prospect or client in place of the marketer.

What follows is a summary and some advice most gurus will not tell you. Incidentally, the very reason gurus who compose these substances so highly urge affiliate advertising is because they're the individuals who create (and benefit from) the goods that lots of affiliates market. By inviting their readers to become affiliate entrepreneurs (particularly because of their merchandise), they construct a digital army of salespeople selling and promoting their e-books, online videos, and classes to their own. Professional internet marketers produce and promote products about online marketing to other people wanting to earn money on the internet. Classes and e-books about online marketing would be the top-rated digital information products bought online. So, let's have a peek at the affiliate enterprise.

Many affiliate programs will have a single commission reimbursement plan. However, some will use a multi-tiered system. Here is the distinction: Just one commission program will cover every affiliate a set percent for every sale that they make via their affiliate website. A multiple mini-program will cover the affiliate a commission to their sales but also will cover a commission on the earnings of affiliates called the principal affiliate. For example, Mary boosts 'Jumpin's Juice' to ABC Company. For every individual that buys a jar of the juice via her site, the provider pays a commission. Mary also promotes other people to market 'Jumpin' Juice.' Joe sees Mary's affiliate connection and needs to be an affiliate. If Joe selects to become an affiliate such as Mary and signals through Mary's site Mary will receive paid a proportion of all of the earnings Joe makes. If a different tier can be obtained, Mary will even make a small percentage over the revenue of these people. Joe signals up. This may sound somewhat like network advertising but allow me to clarify the gap.

Affiliate programs normally will offer a couple of tiers. There'll be a large percentage paid to the affiliates' private sales and a little percentage paid to the 1st grade. One company I am associated with, such as pays me 50 percent in my earnings and 10% over the earnings of those individuals I recruit because of fellow associates. That means that you can view in multi-tiered affiliate programs there isn't a large motivation to perform a great deal of recruitment. It's a great feature, though, so should you happen to inform somebody else about the program, you may earn a bit for doing this. Affiliate programs concentrate on the private sales quantity, not recruitment. Network advertising on the flip side goes past a retailing commission, also highlights the recruitment of others that will equally purchase/sell goods and amuse others that do this. MLMs promote the perpetuation of recruitment by dispersing the commission via multiple tiers (known as amounts).

You can find affiliate programs such as virtual (electronic) products, for example, E-books, etc., and you will find affiliate programs for both solid and services products. Generally, virtual goods cover just one commission. Usually, you'll come across numerous payout tiers through services and products that are solid. You'll also realize that virtual merchandise and services will typically cover you more than powerful goods, occasionally up to 70 percent or even more. Also, typically, you'll get paid from firms whose affiliate applications are handled from the significant affiliate programs. Frequently you will get 2%-5% on many merchandise sales with an occasional 10 percent on vitamins and specific other goods through affiliate programs. Frequently, it isn't worth the work and cost to market those products. The topmost entrepreneurs can expect to make a recurring commission on duplicate purchases of clients they refer although not every item is a repeat purchase, and not every business will provide replicate sales commissions. Advertisers that have triumphed together do so by forcing massive targeted visitors to web pages they have established that inspection or compare goods or solutions. By way of instance, they may construct a web page comparing the various kinds of single-serve espresso coffee manufacturers and then set a buy link for every. Another example where affiliate programs may be helpful is for people who run a main non-product oriented site but will promote a connection to get a product. In any event, enormous volumes of visitors are needed for a little reaction.

A significant thing I wish to highlight about affiliate programs is how they generally won't supply you with recurring earnings. You'll need to always search for, study and examine new products to market to maintain the income flowing. What's popular and quite salable today likely will not be annually (or maybe a week) out of today. Some goods are extremely short-run or timing sensitive. The exclusion of this one-time fee will be affiliate applications for membership websites where you're paid every time your clients renew their subscription. You ought to be aware that member websites have a very large attrition rate; nevertheless (on a typical 60%-90% of individuals will stop within a year), which means you still should constantly promote to continue to keep members coming up to replace the drop-outs.

Why should you bother using affiliate advertising in any way? It could be mainly due to the large proportion payout possible and the capability to make fast. As an example, if you market something which pays you to state, $20 a purchase, and you also sell two a day, you'll find a check for $1200 monthly. And that's simply 1 product. Therefore, if you sell three or four products that sell similar to this, you'd be pulling in three or four times longer. By comparison, an MLM program will require you months or perhaps years to construct a community big enough to create that type of cash. That means it is possible to see the charm and yet another reason why nearly all of the gurus instruct folks affiliate advertising as the main enterprise.

Since I mentioned previously, as an affiliate marketer, you may always have to find new info products to market to maintain a stable income flowing into. Bright affiliates will find highly specialized market solutions. The advertising competition is not as fierce, and because market buyers extremely dedicate to their niched curiosity, they create prospects that are targeted. Also, most market products have an extremely great 'shelf life,' meaning that the item is not as inclined to achieve net saturation, and the data contained less inclined to become rancid. A marketer has produced an extremely comfortable income on the internet simply by locating a bunch of starving market buyers and supplying those individuals with the advice products that they crave.

Internet affiliate advertising networks offer an environment in which businesses that have something to market (Advertisers) meet companies who understand how to market it (Publishers). Many big internet affiliate marketing networks supply countless goods to be offered to their network of tens of thousands of publishers.

Affiliate marketing networks normally work on a performance basis (CPA), in which you pay when a sale or lead will be created for you. You get a sale or guide in a predetermined price and then grant the affiliate system using a bounty for creating the purchase or guide for you. The affiliate network subsequently pays its publishers to generate earnings for your benefit, minus the system retains for itself to putting the deal together. This might seem somewhat like a shopping portal site, but there are many distinct differences. A shopping portal puts your goods in direct relation to the internet shopper. Internet affiliate advertising networks set your merchandise in direct link with publishers (advertising or networking firms). Each writer will subsequently utilize their tools to create earnings for you, make it PPC, SEO, email, and banner ads, and so on.

Not every service or product will operate with an affiliate advertising effort, and lots of affiliate programs won't take your offer unless specific criteria are satisfied. The normal website isn't "marketing prepared" to get an online affiliate advertising effort, and frequently takes a redesign or another site to permit for simple sales or direct conversions. Most sales lead generation campaigns to operate across internet affiliate advertising networks so long as you aren't attempting to accumulate an excessive amount of information, or advice which makes your clients feel nervous like a social security number. For product sales, you want to present an extremely appealing offer such as "that a free 7-day trial to get a daily diet pill," "free solutions for just one month," or whatever which may be thought of as a very low hazard bargain. An offer, for example, a 42-inch plasma display Television for just $1,597, may not do the job. As always, there are exceptions, and you might want to work closely together with your affiliate manager to generate a campaign that is going to be popular among those publishers.

Because of the nature of the affiliate programs, they can be explosive and insecure and aren't suggested for any business until they have lots of online advertising experience under their belt. The general earnings potential of affiliate marketing can be tremendous, and sometimes enormous earnings numbers become involved, so do huge risks. Many affiliate programs have what are called "Super Affiliates" that possess the capability to generate thousands and thousands of dollars in revenue commissions every month. The volatility stems from the advertising power accessible through an affiliate system, alongside the performance-based environment they supply.

For the most part, the publishers that make the sale through the Affiliate networks are covetous. They would like to sell just the services and products which give them the maximum earnings. It's their best, after all, since they're focusing on a performance basis and suppose all advertising dangers. If a fantastic deal comes in an affiliate system, in which a great deal of money may be created, many publishers can promote the merchandise, and earnings will come flowing in. If an item comes from that doesn't generate great or acceptable earnings for the publishers, then they will choose not to advertise the merchandise, and revenue will be nearly nonexistent. It's tricky to locate the ideal balance to fulfill all parties involved (advertiser, writer, affiliate system, and prospective client.) All parties have to be happy to produce an effective affiliate campaign. The swing involving a top-performing effort and an unpopular person may be enormous. This volatility presents a substantial danger, which comes in 3 flavors.

- **Affiliate Network Marketing Risk:**

(1) Not sufficient company you've put considerable resources and time into creating an internet affiliate advertising campaign. You've commissioned all kinds of advertising creative, site design as well as bulked your sales team. Despite this preparation, the supply isn't a moneymaker for those publishers, and they aren't advertising your effort. Your expenditures have grown in expectation of increased earnings that just never materialized.
(2) Too much company you hit the nail on the head. The supply is sexy, and the publishers adore it. They enjoy it so far that earnings flow in quicker than you can deal with. Your call center can manage 50 leads daily; however, the publishers are creating 200. For every sale or guide made, you need to pay a commission whether you can deal with it. You're absolutely downing in an excessive amount of organization, and your pocketbook can not hold out long enough to enlarge so.
(3) Cheating you did not invest much effort in safeguarding your leads or sales. Your internet affiliate advertising effort is generating a lot of leads; however, earnings aren't happening. You're getting numerous disconnected telephone numbers, invalid credit card numbers, or even individuals who say "I signed up to the gift" Leads are coming, but a lot of jagged publishers are still submitting bogus info to receive paid as when their information was actual. Notice the way that previous lead needed a Texas place code their zip code has

been "12345," they said they reside in Alaska and gave the credit card amount "4444555544445555."
Most Internet Affiliate Marketing networks will even ask if they could run your campaign exclusively. This usually means they are the sole affiliate system that may supply your offer into the world. There are a few different advantages and disadvantages to conducting your effort exclusively with a single system.

- **Exclusive Affiliate community Campaign Benefits:**

Your supervisor of the internet affiliate marketing campaign can pass your effort on to other internet affiliate advertising networks, and also manage your accounts for you. This saves you considerable time with not needing to find new programs, organizing effort launches, advertising creative, along with other activities necessary to establish a new effort.

You won't need to pay startup charges or sign contracts to the affiliate advertising networks your affiliate manager enters your effort online to. You merely work beneath your only agreement with your affiliate manager. This can help save you thousands of dollars in startup costs and a great deal of time.

Affiliate advertising networks utilize exclusive efforts since "bragging rights," and frequently give priority for their private campaigns. Your effort is far more likely to be promoted into the publishers and also given particular attention. This can help to get your effort noticed from the writer, and finally boosts sales or direct flow.

Exclusive Affiliate network Cons:

Your campaign supervisor will outsource your effort to other internet affiliate advertising networks. Precisely, you won't know who's promoting your deal, and so the grade of the internet traffic coming to your site is not unknown.

Your affiliate supervisor might not be as challenging as you. Your effort might not have passed to other internet affiliate advertising networks; also, as it's a private offer, you cannot pass it to other sites. Growth might become stifled.

The publishers that run your effort through outsourced affiliate programs won't get as large in a payout (sales commission). There are essentially two affiliate advertising networks: The affiliate system, along with the network that is publicized. More hands are at the pot, making money and leaving for the publishers. The diminished publisher with lead to diminished interest in your effort, therefore the outsourced online affiliate advertising networks won't be as successful as though you worked together directly.

Most affiliate programs will want to integrate email advertising into your effort. That is highly recommended, as revenue or lead production volumes might be significantly greater. Should you allow your effort to become an email promoted, you'll have to have the ability to keep an email correction list. The suppression record is a listing of email addresses of all folks that wish to opt-out from getting your deal. An e-mail has to be supplied in your email advertising imaginative where people can opt-out out of the offer. You should then provide the suppression document into your affiliate community so that they can consequently move your suppression file for your publishers. This is part of Can-Spam law; also, it may be efficiently handled with a little opt-out landing page attached to a very simple database. Ensure that you provide an upgraded suppression file into the affiliate programs at least one time each week.

- **Launching affiliate advertising campaigns which Combine:**

You aim to create a campaign that places the most money possible to your writer's pockets, while also creating for yourself. Remember, a break-even effort is also a successful effort provided that you're able to re-market for your clientele and create extra sales, updates, etc.

However, layout your effort to maximize conversions, reduce the clicks necessary to buy an item, or have your lead generation typed on your home page. Do not collect information which you truly don't want, or people don't want to distribute (such as an SSN). You might need to construct an exceptional site for the internet affiliate advertising campaign if your present site isn't appropriate for affiliate advertising.

You're competing against each one of the other campaigns in an affiliate system, not only ones promoting the same item you're. Publishers maximize the supplies they promote and shed bad performing attempts. Layout an offer that functions both for you and your publishers; your affiliate manager may provide help.

Create the measures essential to permit your effort to become an email promoted by the publishers. This usually means you'll have to make Can-Spam compliant email advertising imaginative, an easy-to-use webpage connected into your database, and supply access to an upgraded suppression file (a text dump of your database partitioning document). Email advertising will greatly enhance your effort's effectiveness.

Create a massive variety of different marketing creative, tons of standard size banner ads, several email inventive, multiple email names and subject lines, different text links, and so forth. Your affiliate supervisor will supply you a listing of crucial media forms and dimensions, but attempt to supply greater than their minimum requirements.

Keep together with direct fraud and quality. No matter how complex your investigation system can get, somebody will attempt to steal bogus data beyond you. Be certain you could monitor all lead resources, such as the sub IDs which are passed through the affiliate system.

Every single time you create an alteration to your site, submit an examination to make sure the affiliate effort is still operating as it needs to be. If your site has a mistake preventing revenue conversions or poses monitoring issues, you might be requested to cover the publishers to get their lost business. Bear in mind your broken site will influence many businesses who stuck their neck out to you.

Be ready for large quantities of prospects, or no prospects in any way.

The dangers associated with affiliate system advertising would be numerous, and they are important. You have to be on your feet, thinking forward and fast to maneuver in case things turn sour. But should you come ready and designing an offer the publishers adore, the monetary rewards could be huge.

- **How to Start**

We have broken down the process into seven measures for internet affiliate advertising beginners. After this guide will put you on the ideal path and have you making your very first commission very quickly.

1. Decide on a Niche
Before you begin building your first Website, you'll want to choose which niche you are likely to goal.

If you do not understand what your Website is about or that you likely aim onto it, you cannot really build a website about it; can you?

If you have already figured out this one, the way to go, this is undoubtedly among the toughest and overwhelming measures.

If you do not exactly know what your market is, nevertheless, here is some information which you may discover useful.

Some important questions to consider when deciding your Market are:

What matters am I passionate about?
It is easier to work on a thing if you are passionate about it. Plus, whenever you've got a fire, you are usually very knowledgeable about it also, so that helps. As an instance, when you've got a fire about cosmetics, your market of selection may be makeup associated, also.

Can there be cash in this market?
While following your fire is unquestionably the recommended alternative, on occasion, the potential for earning money in a booming market trumps passion. Thus, you may not always understand much about your specialty, but when it is very likely to earn you cash, you could always find out more about it?

By way of example, KitchenFaucetDivas is a Website that was constructed for gain, not fire. Unless, of course, there's a person out there having a severe enthusiasm for kitchen faucets! RRB

What subject could I find myself readily writing 25, 50, or 100 blog articles about?

The topic you select should have sufficient depth, in which you can create a lot of articles because of it. This is essential for constructing an authoritative website for research engine optimization, and above all, for your end-user. If you do not have sufficient content about a subject, you are not likely to be taken quite seriously as an authority on the subject, and it is unlikely you could convince a person to create a buy from you.

MoneySavingExpert is a superb example of a website with a subject. For that, you'd have a never-ending source of articles thoughts.

Can there be room within this market for one more affiliate marketer?
Many profitable niches are also quite popular among affiliate advertising (e.g., weight reduction), but before leaping on-board using a hugely common market, make certain that there's enough space for you. That's, are you in a position to generate income and compete with established entrepreneurs? Otherwise, keep searching.

Can there be sufficient attention in/demand for goods within this market?
The market you select might draw interest out of your audience in regards to studying and obtaining wisdom, but are they ready to purchase important products also? Without customer interest in goods, your market is not likely to make you a lot of money.

Are there any affiliate programs out there in this market?
That is a vital aspect to think about. You may produce a concept for a market you understand a good deal about; however, are there affiliate applications to your market? No affiliate application, no earnings; time to try to find a different market.

2. Research Affiliate Programs
As soon as you've decided on a market, it is time to discover what is out there concerning products and programs to market. You have likely done a little bit of study to this while exploring your market today. You have to dig deeper.

Deciding upon an affiliate application will require a while, but do not be reluctant to commit a large quantity of time to it since this is where your earnings will come out. Deciding upon the right app will ensure it is well worth your time!

When choosing an affiliate System, keep these key things in your head:

What sorts of retailers utilize the app/affiliate system?
Now you want to make certain; other similar vendors are also utilizing the system since this will be able to help you judge your probability of succeeding with the specific program.

Just how much commission are you going to create from the merchandise?
Ensure you register for programs that are rewarding and create a decent return in the investment. A few hints:

When utilizing ClickBank, merchandise ought to have more than a 50 percent commission (rather 60 percent), and also possess a higher gravity score (meaning they are in demand).
For CPA (cost-per-action) apps, commissions ought to be 1, and goods should not be too restrictive in the way you're able to promote them.
For real goods, start looking for commissions around $40.
Would you like to be connected with the Services and Products?
The services and products you'll be boosting to your audience have to be relevant and decent quality. Be certain to think in them and understand them since this is crucial for you bringing the sales pitch for your viewers. You have to build confidence with your viewers, so be certain the services and products that you opt to market are reliable enough.

Ads such as the one under frequently result in sketchy goods do you would like to get connected with something which guarantees effects that may or might not be accurate?

What type of service does the program offer?
Make sure you check what sort of customer service you can expect from the affiliate program as soon as you've signed up. Do your research on the internet and, if at all possible, talk to other vendors using the app to receive their ideas. Would you talk to a person via

Skype or phone, or do you need to wait 72 hours for email answers? Be clear with this and trust me, you'll require support at the same point or another.

3. Build a Website

Measures 1 and 2 are about search and figuring out how and what is potential and rewarding. Now, it is time to begin placing your study into action.

Assuming you do not already have a site built, this may be another step. Luckily, constructing a website is not too complex or labor-intensive since it had been previously.

If you are a newcomer to building websites, the easiest way to establish a website is by using Twitter. Even the WordPress CMS is quite simple to use, and while communicating abilities can be convenient, for the most part, you won't demand any technical knowledge to prepare your website.

You have to follow a couple of actions to get your Website up and running:

Purchase a domain name.
Your domain name is your address for your site (e.g., Www.affilorama.com), so that will be the very first step you'll have to do when establishing your website. Considering that there are a large number of sites on the World Wide Web, it is likely that the domain name that you need may already be obtained by somebody else. So be certain to have a lot of choices in mind. Make certain to browse our guidance on the best way to select a great domain.

There are lots of places you can purchase a domain name, including our own Affilorama Domain support. Other famous choices are GoDaddy along with NameCheap.

Buy and set up hosting.
If your domain name is the speech, hosting is similar to the real house within that your website will reside. It is your very own little piece of the net -- the location where all of your site files reside. Hosting is quite affordable nowadays, and thus don't unnecessarily

scrimp on prices. Proceed with a dependable supplier because your internet affiliate advertising company is dependent upon it.

Some cheap and reliable hosting suppliers we urge are GoDaddy, HostGator along with BlueHost.

If you buy your domain name and hosting from various businesses, you'll have to join both together. Do not panic; it is an easy procedure. Check out our suggestion: Joining your Domain Names with your Hosting.

Install WordPress.
After your hosting has been installed, you have to set up a content management system (CMS) to your website. We advocate WordPress since it's not difficult to use, and also, a newcomer (like you!) can very quickly find out how it functions. Most hosting providers are going to have a one-click install alternative for WordPress, so it is only going to take you a couple of minutes, and you'll get WordPress installed on your website.

Put in your motif.
A WordPress theme supplies all of the stylings of a Website that you (and your audience) view about. There are hundreds and hundreds of subjects available; therefore, picking one may seem daunting initially. Our information: choose something simple and easy to personalize. You could always change it afterward.

AffiloTheme is a fantastic alternative. Entirely customizable, and constructed especially for affiliate marketers, you may use this WordPress theme to skip a lot of the first learning curve additional affiliate marketers will probably encounter. You might even hunt for topics on a website such as Theme Forest.

Produce articles.
Ultimately, once your Website is prepared, it is time to make content to it. The information you produce has to be related to your market but also intriguing and engaging enough to keep your viewers coming back. It's also advisable to guarantee that the website content is a hunt engine.

4. Create Excellent Content

Now your Website is installed, and you have joined an affiliate program, you are prepared to start perhaps the very time-consuming (but possibly rewarding) portion of this affiliate company: Producing content.

This is where the overused, however, truer-than-ever term "content is king" comes in to play.

Your aim for your Website is to set it as an Authority website in your specialty, and the chief means to get this done is to always create unique, high-quality articles.

This could include:

Product testimonials
Your affiliate website version could be established off composing testimonials about various services or products. That is a frequent version, and, when done well, can prove quite beneficial in generating affiliate revenue.

By way of example, the Cable Cutter is concentrated on writing reviews of several distinct sorts of merchandise and assisting their subscribers to make the best choice regarding the merchandise they wish to purchase. After reading an overview of their website, when the consumer clicks through the product/service utilizing the affiliate website, Wire Cutter will make a commission out of it - website posts that tackle common difficulties, queries, or problems applicable to your intended marketplace.
Creating blog articles is a very helpful and effective way of consistently building articles on a website. When generating blog posts, it is a fantastic idea to do a little keyword research to determine what it is that your audience is most interested in and looking for on the internet. Moreover, make certain to research opponents, forums, and societal websites to narrow down on themes to your site.

By way of example, Security Guard Coaching HQ has an extremely comprehensive blog on many different topics relevant for anybody interested in safety guard training, tasks, and much more.

Evergreen articles
If you're building a Website with the capacity for information that will not age and stay useful for the audience, you've got the chance to produce what's called evergreen content. It is important to perform comprehensive keyword research before planning any Wordpress material for a website similar to this since your website could tremendously benefit from the right use of keywords inside this article.

By way of example, the articles on Super Weddings are helpful whether you are arranging a wedding now or a year ago. All of the content on the website is made accordingly. It's split into groups to make it rather easier and suitable for your readers or viewers to get what they're searching for. This is also quite great for SEO.

Informational merchandise
Giving out free informational merchandise like an e-book, an email, a mini-course is a favorite approach many affiliate marketers utilize. Normally, your subscribers might need to supply their email addresses to obtain the item from you. After that, you can use this to market to them through email advertising. Furthermore, an informational item may create curiosity about the true product you are attempting to sell. In case your merchandise is hot enough and attracts enough visitors to your website, you might additionally monetize the traffic in different ways, like AdSense.

A fantastic illustration is DatingMetrics, in which you are enticed with a Free Texting Crash Course in trade to your email address. The actual advertising will start when the consumer has downloaded this program.

The kind of material you make for your Site will largely rely on your specialty, as particular kinds of content function better in certain markets than many others.

Understand: Purchasing generic content isn't an effective system to construct your website. While it might be tempting to replicate your website such as this, in the very long term, it will not enable you to place yourself as an authority in your market (and finally means fewer visitors and fewer earnings).

5. Construct an audience

Assembling a viewer for your Website can, in certain ways, follow naturally as soon as you get started producing exceptional content. A curious audience is not only going to bring you consistent traffic but also cause consistent earnings for you.

So how do you start creating a viewer to get a Brand new website? Below are a few thoughts:

- Boost your articles through social networking

The simplest and most frequent way to begin constructing an audience to get a site is through social networking. Based on your specialty and business, you can pick out of Facebook, Twitter, Instagram, Pinterest, and lots of other market and location-specific networks. Building an engaged and curious following on interpersonal networking is a fantastic chance to construct relationships, and after you have their confidence, market your services and products to them.

I will utilize MoneySavingExpert.com, for instance. The Website has over 154,000 enjoys on its own Facebook webpage and its links with the crowd by discussing hyperlinks to articles but also requesting money-saving/budgeting associated queries. The exceptionally engaged readers subsequently pay a visit to the web site, where they browse articles without doubts making buys.

- Guest article on a high tech blog

While your Website is still fresh, it is a fantastic idea to get started capitalizing on somebody else's crowd. Continue focusing on constructing your content, but also contemplating writing content to get a couple of large, high-traffic blogs that are applicable for your specialty. By composing articles for a larger website, you can have in front of some other crowd and showcase your experience on a certain topic. This will gradually cause more visitors to your website, too.

- Construct an email list

Let nobody tell you that email advertising is lifeless. An email list is vital for every single affiliate marketer. It's possible to begin building your email list using an outcome magnet (such as the advice products mentioned above) or perhaps by simply inviting your audience to register for your updates. You may then push your articles to the audience through email and direct them to your affiliate provides. Do not be sleazy in regards to the earnings, but if you develop enough confidence with your email crowd, if the moment comes, they won't mind buying a product from you.

- Utilize fundamental SEO methods to improve search engine visitors to your website.

Organic research remains a significant source of visitors for any site. Therefore you must optimize your site to search engines too. When creating your articles, you have to always, thus keep your reader in mind, but do not neglect to stick to a few basic search engine optimization principles too.

Learn SEO yourself or employ a fantastic Search Engine Optimization marketer to assist you to optimize off-page and on-page search engine optimization chances for your website. If your website begins to show up in search results in phrases applicable to your market, it is going to be a massive boost towards creating your viewers (along with your earnings)!

- Invest in paid advertisements.

Many affiliate marketers utilize paid advertising to create extra visitors to their website and drive more revenue. Paid advertisement on interpersonal media is frequently a fantastic place to begin because these networks tend to be affordable. You might also need to think about taking out cheap banner advertisements on little market websites. Based upon your specialty, Google AdWords might also be a fantastic choice to drive a few paid visitors to your website.

6. Boost Affiliate Offers

At length, the part we have been waiting for!

That, my friends, is where things kick into top gear. Many fly-by-night franchisees will leap directly to the measure and skip measures 1--5 fully. And that is what's going to set you apart.

As soon as you've revealed that you can provide something of value to your market, it is time to keep on adding value by boosting products that are going to be helpful and useful to your viewers.

You can market your offers in several means. It will rely on the sort of site you have built and what you are selling. Some ideas include:

· Product testimonials

Compose fair, genuine reviews about goods. Build up confidence together with your audience, and bear in mind they rely upon your view. Do not just point out all of the advantages of merchandise and gloss over the disadvantages. An honest opinion is going to be appreciated. Add persuasive images and produce mention of helpful features, specifications, and other specifics.

Your product review may then connect to the webpage (along with your Affiliate ID attached), where your audience may create a purchase if they are interested, so if you do, hooray! You have created your first purchase.

Banners advertising

You can set up banners on your Website to market your affiliate offers. Many affiliate programs will typically offer their creativity once you register for their offers. All you need to do is add the banner ads on an extremely trafficked page (your affiliate monitoring is generally embedded inside the code). Banner advertisements in the ideal places can do a fantastic job of forcing earnings.

Below are some examples of banner ads that Templatic supplies to its affiliates.

In-text articles links.

This is a really common means to advertise supplies. For instance, you may often find a blog article with links to specific products or solutions. In case the reader clicks through and makes a purchase, then the website owner will create a commission. These in-text hyperlinks blend in with additional articles on your website and are an excellent means of boosting an offer inside your content without even being over-the-top sales using banners.

Mail promotions.
For those who have built an email list, then you can also promote your affiliate provides through email promotions. Just be certain that you develop a connection with your audience instead of going to the hard sell straightaway. The mails that you send out should include your affiliate links to products; therefore, whenever your viewers click through. The purchase is credited to you.

Reviews and giveaways
Lots of affiliate programs will frequently run promotions with great giveaways or discounts, which may be appealing to your viewers. By way of instance, if you are an Amazon associate along with the website, have a sizable Holiday Sale, it could be the ideal chance for you to market discounts for your site traffic. This is a superb way to market your supplies while also providing very good value to your viewers.

When marketing affiliate provides, make certain, you're fully conscious of all of the stipulations attached to an affiliate application. Some applications can be stringent about how they let you market their merchandise. By way of instance, some can restrict you to banner advertisements and hyperlinks only, while some are going to allow you to utilize paid advertisements, but will not allow email advertising.

Also, make certain you have a disclaimer in your site that advises your viewers, which you might have hyperlinks that encourage affiliate offers. This is essential for many affiliate programs in addition to a fundamental courtesy of your site traffic. In the U.S., the FTC mandates disclosure for affiliate marketers (and anybody trapping endorsements), too.

7. Rinse, lather, also Duplicate
Now that you are done with steps 1 - 6, step 7 is to keep doing what you are doing. Yes, badly!

Your continuing function as an affiliate marketer is to repeat steps 4 - 6 to a consistent basis. Building a website till a place where it could cause you to get consistent earnings requires a little bit of effort, and you ought to be happy to constantly make, market, promote, innovate and naturally, promote.

Overview of Key Points
It may feel overwhelming to perform all of the essential work Involved in establishing your website and building your standing. But trust me, as soon as you've created that initial purchase, all of the hard work would be well worth it!

To sum up, making your initial affiliate commission takes a little bit of work, but if you break down it and follow along step by step, it will not seem so overpowering in any way. Following is a fast recap of everything you have to do:

- Pick your specialty.
- Make research on affiliate programs and merchandise.
- Construct a Website.
- Create excellent content.
- Construct a viewer.
- Boost your affiliate product(s).
- Repeat steps #47 to a continuous basis!

As you can see, there's a tried-and-true approach when it comes to affiliate marketing to novices. Put at the job, and you will quickly be reaping the benefits of your very first sale.

CHAPTER FIVE
AMAZON FBA

Straightforward access, infinite selection, and speedy processing are a number of those infinite charms of e-commerce. When tapped intelligently, these variables can be both valuable both for sellers and buyers. To be able to draw buyers and revel in massive earnings, online traders need to meet widely expected requisites of e-commerce. Assessing all market needs and remaining focused on every facet of your company can be feverish for any e-merchant. Sometimes, you want to acquire additional assistance to arrange your regular company and to easily conduct all of its operations. Fulfillment from Amazon is just one such resourceful internet service that offers a supporting hand to retailers by professionally executing the sensitive and complex purchase fulfillment process on their behalf.

Fulfillment from Amazon (FBA) is also an extremely functional application designed to provide vendors with all the storage facilities to get their stock and implement requests from Amazon satisfaction center. In almost any e-commerce, prepared storage and continuous satisfaction are critically essential for overall business growth, client satisfaction, and profit maximization. FBA presents people and tiny businesses in addition to large businesses with the chance to surpass the expectations of the clients with secure, smart, and quick purchase shipping. But if you're a producer or a wholesaler, then you can pay full attention for your buying and manufacturing since by availing FBA, you're no longer needed to keep your warehouse and endure hefty placement price. You do not even need to be concerned about product packaging and dispatch, no matter the frequency or size of these orders.

Send products to Amazon

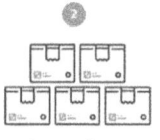
Amazon stores products

Customers purchase

Amazon picks up products

Amazon ships products

The machine of Fulfillment from Amazon may seem complex, but in practice, it is very straightforward to follow because it's solidly made, keeping in mind real trading requirements and newest e-commerce tendencies. As soon as you've sent your new or used merchandise to the satisfaction center, they're stored in Amazon storehouses in prepared to send shape. Amazon initiates order gratification to your goods upon receiving requests from clients through its site or on your direct petition for their dispatch. This process is followed closely by the uplifting of the given items from stock to then packing them for shipment. At length, the ordered products are sent from Amazon satisfaction centers into the stated destinations. Following the deduction of gratification fees, the net sale amount is credited to your accounts, and also the same procedure is repeated for the following trades. You can rest assured that each one of the actions involved is done mechanically seamlessly in a professional way from the most reliable, efficient, and seasoned hands of Amazon.

It's nonetheless very important to note that shares under FBA always stay under the seller's possession and management. Because there are no lower or upper stock constraints, you can include or draw your merchandise from satisfaction shops whenever you prefer. In the same way, purchase frequency isn't significant at all due satisfaction charges are just deducted at the point of purchase. A number of the other fantastic attributes of FBA comprise personalized order processing, insurance, and automatic tracking. In the long run, it may be reasoned that Fulfillment from Amazon highlights that you ought to focus on your creation, sales, and direction without being concerned a dime regarding order fulfillment.

Amazon FBA, also normally selling goods around the Amazon platform, now has become a goldmine for quite a few vendors - that got early and managed to nurture an audience that wanted what they had been offering.

To do so correctly, you must have the ability to consider just what you're doing concerning the selling of merchandise, and the way they are showcased.

Aside from appealing photographs, the explanation is the primary way people can acquire an insight into just what the product does, how it operates - and how it's different from some other rival ones.

This tutorial intends to highlight the way you can handle the most successful Amazon product list descriptions.

- **Construction**

Amazon product listings stick to the identical structure:

Name
Pictures
Characteristics (Bullet Points)
Description (incl HTML)
What most People today see at the Amazon list is the very best part (Name, Images & Bullet Points) - that the "beef" of this list is your description, which may contain basic HTML formatting.

If you would like to create an effective record, then the trick is to be more apparent, concise, and comprehensive.

The top generally possess clear, higher definition graphics, coupled with insightful & persuasive bullet points (that are concentrated on rewards) plus a keyword-rich name)

The actual killer the "backup" employed through the list. The two from the bullet-points and also the entire description, having the ability to communicate the advantages of the item while ensuring that the reader is forced to purchasing your distinct product, is a nice line.

Because of the character of the backup, a range of copywriting specialists have been making serious cash supplying "Amazon Product Listing" copywriting solutions. The assumption is that they are going to help people earn more money by writing more lucid backup.

- **The Way to Make It Yourself**

As stated, the above structure is pretty-much what decides if an item is going to be approved by Amazon.

The most important thing to do is know what "causes" buyers to trust your merchandise.

When selling goods, it is much better to take care of emotion than logic.

Logically, you might believe the item could be recorded, and individuals will select it, assess it according to its attributes, and make a buy.
Emotionally, folks choose products from the business they believe will provide an experience as near to their dreams as you can.
Such examples like creating a "persuasive" name (which only must record the several characteristics of this item from the view of how it may be utilized) and a "description" that showcases the way the item can fit in the purchaser's lifetime will convert considerably greater than just listing the qualities of the goods. Bear in mind, and nearly all individuals are purchasing the merchandise for an ulterior reason, stressing how it may drive them to the inherent result is likely to produce the difference between purchasing the solution or not.

For the end, the next describes how all the components of this description function:

Title

The most important thing to make sure using a product's name is that it is as descriptive as you can.

Some goods (like books) do not need too descriptive titles. On the other hand, nearly all classes do need the most descriptive name potential.

Think about the following illustrations:

AYL Silicone Cooking Gloves - Heat Resistant Oven Mitt for Grilling, BBQ, Kitchen - Safe Handling of Pots and Pans - Cooking & Baking Non-Slip Potholders - Inner Protective Cotton Layer
AYL Silicone Cooking Gloves (Green) - Heat Resistant Oven Mitt + Internal Cotton Layer
It is demonstrated the best title extends higher.

The cause of this is very easy folks hope that the more descriptive nature of this.

In a clean of 100's of comparable products, people need quality, significance, and security, the firm behind the product, is likely to be valid. Possessing a descriptive, comprehensive name at the best one is among the very best methods to get it done.

Pictures

Pictures are essential for receiving products detected.

The keys, together with images, will be as follows:

Clarity is everything* do not be concerned about any desktop or anything - people wish to determine the quality of the goods and anticipate 4k+ vision to reveal it.
Just show what needed software products do not "want" a box, but they will increase the awareness of its caliber of individuals who mostly have to determine screenshots
Ensure the images signify *precisely * what the purchaser is becoming - do not utilize any tricks/hacks to make the product seem much better than what it is - only show folks the item & accessories that might include it.
If you are not quite good at photos, you are going to want to speak with a photographer.

Alternately, there are companies on the likes of Fiverr who will be able to prepare a fantastic shot too.

The purpose is that so long as you've got ~5 very good pictures, this ought to be fine.

Characteristics (Bullet Points)

That is where things begin to acquire importantly.

The attributes (bullet points) are all meant to describe the specifications of the merchandise; they are now mainly utilized to supply users with info regarding the item (replicate).

Whatever you compose, there are numerous components to contemplate:

Wrap attributes inside advantages - instead of stating "15cm extended," state "3 HANDY SIZES - 5cm, 10cm & 15cm"
Include all five bullets - may be tempting to use three - utilize all the five and also discuss the business & "warranty" for the previous 1
Fight "CAPITALIZED" advantages - buyers wish to understand what the item is about to for them, then - you do so together with "CAPITALIZED TITLES - accompanied by an explanation of every stage."
Do not be reluctant to utilize several paragraphs for every bullet a few products require the features recorded; should you require more advantage, add replicate.
Concentrate on the item (not the buyer) - novices make the mistake of leading with buyer-centric advantages (since they read it into the certain copywriting discussion) - that is awful. Individuals are about Amazon to get goods, not find out about how a toaster glove will cause them to seem younger.
As mentioned, if you are taking a look at creating a successful strategy, you have to have the ability to promote buyers to your business - and from virtue - your goods are dependable and higher quality.

- **How you do this would be to create as much use of their accessible content area as you can.**

Description

Last, the description will be that the majority of content under all of the specifications layout "above the fold."

Based on the type of merchandise, and if you've got a brand new brand or an established firm, the "description" place could be quite a range of various things.

It is ideal to think about it like some item list page on eBay, defying what is available precisely. Minus pictures, a Similar condition of affairs is different (you can use limited quantities of HTML inside).

The most important thing to understand is that you are not limited to only bullet-points (because you're with the product attributes) that not only gives slightly more creative liberty. This usually means that you will need to be certain you're making the ideal decisions.

Fight together using the SINGLE reason people would purchase your product over a competitor's - advertising/revenue 101, but it is really simple to overlook it. There is a SINGLE reason people purchase a specific product (it may function as quality, layout or the way it functions)
Lead using a headline, then use a little bit of blurb to describe the merchandise and use a few bullet points to explain what the purchaser will exactly get you to receive ~300 words and thus don't go-ahead.
Select an emotive angle - the very best merchandises are offered via emotion use backup that elicits thoughts of the way the item will fit right into somebody's lifetime.
Use HTML sparingly bold text is so fine, but maybe not the defining variable of the product do not go forward with all the stylization (it must highlight the replicate, not specify it)
What advantages do you expect in an FBA enterprise?
An e-commerce firm usually browses through the Producers of meeting orders and shipping goods to its clients in a timely way. Using the power of Amazon, you will take that specific challenge from your working equation.

Another sophistication of an e-commerce shop is keeping tabs of stock and receiving products recorded. Employing the FBA business design, you send the goods into Amazon's warehouse and permit them to look after the remainder.

With both of these challenges from the way, the direction of your company and expansion takes off as:

• You're free to concentrate your attention on greater degree tasks such as conversion optimization (CRO), targeted advertising, and growing new markets.

• There are lots of Amazon perks by which you both and your clients can profit. Managing charge cards, fast delivery, free delivery, and customer support are only a number of those advantages.

• Development opportunities are built in an FBA Enterprise model. You're focused on development instead of pursuing orders.

• Lower costs are another advantage. You cannot warehouse or boat from a personal e-business at precisely the same speed which you get with Amazon's facilities.

Even though an FBA company if far from becoming hands-free, it does up you against the busywork of a company and permits you to concentrate on those jobs that can produce growth and advancement.

How much could you make from an FBA enterprise?
That is a difficult question to answer because there are so many factors involved. But, you will find FBA company proprietors that have made anyplace from $3,000 to 40,000 over the initial 30 days of launching their FBA company.

Others have gone in the earnings amount of $0 $50,000 a month in 8 weeks. These are not typical outcomes, but they're a sign of this explosive potential that beginning an FBA company can possess.

The chance exists to make a five, six, or more seven-figure income using an FBA company design and to leverage the power of Amazon.

- **How to Start**

Now that we've got you properly heated up and eager about this fantastic chance with some wonderful revenue potential, let us get down to the job of having your FBA Company began. These are just seven actionable measures with loads of suggestions and practical ideas for the best way best to take them out there. All you need to do is follow along to acquire your FBA Company ready to go.

Step One: Develop an Amazon Seller Account
You can't have an FBA company without producing an Amazon Seller Account. Theoretically, you can save yourself this measure for afterward, but in case you've made a choice to "do that thing," then you may too dedicate yourself by making an account. Here is how:

• Proceed to Amazon's site and scroll towards the bottom of this page at which the page footers are.

• The 2nd daring column in the left is tagged, "Make Cash with us."

• Beneath that going is a connection with the tag "Economy on Amazon."

• Click on that link and then follow the instructions.

Person vs. Skilled

You will need to make an upfront decision regarding whether you want to put up yourself as a person or as an expert. Here's the gap between both:

• A single account won't have a monthly subscription fee. But as it's a free account, you will find a lot of limitations you will be subject to.

• An expert account will have a monthly subscription cost of $39.99, but you also will not be billed for your first month at the same time you get your account setup. The constraints of the account won't shackle you.
If you're playing about, just like if you're a child using a lemonade stand or just like you're hosting a garage sale, then the personal account is nice, but somebody who wants to construct an FBA

company should go directly into the expert accounts and then start things off an.

Measure Two: Select Your Niche
This is nearly the hardest aspect of establishing your FBA Company because when you're excited about a chance, you are inclined to need to market all you can get your hands on. The ideal approach to select your specialty and attempt to ascertain how you're likely to fit in the e-commerce world be to adhere to a structured strategy. Here are the measures to this strategy:

• Contemplate the areas that you're most enthusiastic around and write them from a listing. These can lead to hobbies, special interests, specialist adventures, items you've read about a great deal, or completed an extensive study on, etc. They could come out of, and ought to come out, almost everywhere if you're genuinely thinking outside the box.

• Brainstorm all the Probable goods and Product lines that you may have the ability to provide in every one of these regions. Compose the product and product lines beneath every one of the regions you're enthusiastic about.

• Start narrowing down these lists to quite particular niches. A fantastic example is somebody who loves gardening. Nicely, "gardening provides" is very general in regards to advertising, which means you are going to want to narrow it down into something such as "garden weeding tools," or even "designer flower pots."

• Narrow your listing of markets down to 3 to 4 five places that you're enthusiastic about.

By picking things, places of markets, or interest that you're enthusiastic about, you'll be more excited and educated when it is time to write advertising copy, merchandise listings, blog articles, or introducing a podcast. When you've got items narrowed down a little, proceed onto the next measure.

Measure Three: Research Products

That is where, because they state, "that the Rubber meets the road" although you're certainly enthusiastic about your markets and your goods, creating a business from supplying those products to customers is an entirely different potential. You'll have to do product research from these areas of markets and interest on your lists. Here are some practical measures for conducting product search:

General Product Searches

In this measure, you need to do some basic searches to acquire a better idea of the way the products on your market are represented from the area of e-commerce. Begin with conducting searches to your products on Amazon, eBay, and other leading retail outlets. A fantastic short-cut is to perform a Google search of your merchandise to exactly see what retail outlets manage your chosen goods or comparable ones. If you notice your merchandise normally lists between $10 and $50, then you're on the ideal path. Products involving both of these price points are usually impulse purchases. That is great, as you'll have the ability to turn over a greater quantity of inventory.

- **Utilizing Merchant Words, Jungle Scout and Much Keyword Tools**

This is a keyword tool that's a vital component in specifying the degree of need for your goods. You may use these instruments to observe how frequently your goods are contained in keyword searches, to find out if there's a "great market" for whatever you plan to market.

Whatever some economic theorists state, and provide, demand push the marketplace on every item, service, and source; items in demand market in a greater volume in addition to a greater cost, based on how a lot of these things are readily available. Ideally, you need your merchandise to maintain high demand, however maybe not possess a lot of suppliers providing exactly the very same products.

Greatest Seller Rankings (BSR)

Amazon BSR must not be the Maximum priority for Determining if you market a specific product or maybe not; however, they do provide you with a peek into which goods and which product groups tend to attract the most buyers. Have a look at the initial three to five goods on the BSR over the numerous markets and categories to which you've narrowed your listing. A reduce BSR number usually means that more of that specific thing is selling compared to its rivals. Whether there are a high number of goods with reduced BSR in a specific product class, then you're in a very competitive class. Categories with greater BSR positions make it a ton simpler to break in the market along with your first product listings.

Added Programs for Market Research

There are some very powerful tools for performing much more In-depth market study, which may offer you with plenty of information in addition to how to translate it. Among the most famous and highly effective FBA market study software is Jungle Scout. Other market research programs include:

• AMZ Scout. • AMZ Base. • Sonar • Watched Item (which monitors things on eBay) • Unicorn Smasher.

FBA prices

After you've narrowed your product listing to some choice things or a merchandise class, you are going to want to consult with Amazon's tools to learn which degree of FBA prices are related to that specific item. These charges depend upon numerous unique factors linked to the item's dimensions, shape, and weight, specific storage, or specific handling. You are going to want to attempt and maintain these FBA penalties as minimum as you can to keep your expenses down.

Added Product Research Tips

In case you have faithfully followed the steps above, you need to have narrowed your products down a little from this huge brainstorm list that you began with. Now, you may be prepared to start into another step. However, there are some more things that you may wish to think about if you're still unsure about what products will fit your company objectives. Consider these additional suggestions:

• Avoid competing with all well-established products and highly established brand names. Competing with the big boys won't get the job done nicely with you. They've marketing strategies and marketing and advertising budgets that you cannot compete with.

• Contemplate volume items or clearance items out of retail stores. This permits you to sell new name goods and develop your company in the brief term. It's tricky to maintain a constant supply of those products coming, and therefore don't base your whole FBA company on this form of strategy.

• You can find out things in local retail shops as a way of market study too. To try it, you are going to want to create use of a recorder scanning program in your Smartphone, such as the Amazon Sellers program or Scoutify program.

From the time you've worked through all the measures and utilized a few of the extra strategies for advertising study, you ought to have shown your market and the chief product or goods where you need to direct off.

Step Four: Establish Product Sourcing
Placing your initial product and product lines is just half the battle; however, you need yet another step to consider before it is possible to begin selling and listing goods. You need to set up the sourcing of all your merchandise. Without merchandise sourcing, so you still do not have a thing to market. This can be a rather time-consuming process as you are going to want to acquire the most trustworthy supplier with the maximum quality of merchandise out there.

Testing Products

In case you have used the products you would like to market, then you may not have to do some testing. But if you're taking a look at generic marketplace things to save expenses, you will surely need to be certain you are still supplying the highest quality of merchandise potential to your clientele. You are going to want to get your hands on several samples of those products before deciding whether you're receiving quality merchandise sourcing.

Locate a Provider

Typically, price is what's going to determine which provider best matches your requirements as sourcing to your merchandise. Here are many different avenues for finding a provider for your goods:

• Overseas Providers. Lots of FBA Company owners are going to use sources away from the U.S., such as Alibaba, that may produce bulk purchases of goods in 25 percent or less compared to the standard retail cost. Sourcing in the international wholesaler enables you a wider profit margin.

• Local Trade Shows. Find local trade shows that host business leaders who offer the products you'll be sourcing at a wholesale cost. Look for trade displays online, through trade publications and papers.

• Bulk and Clearance Items from Neighborhood Retailers. We talked about this earlier because of a potential short term sourcing.

• Neighborhood generates. In case you happen to be promoting a product that's created locally, by all means, use local producers as a way of sourcing your merchandise. They're sure to enjoy your efforts.

You will want to establish a fantastic relationship with your providers, particularly if they have extra items that may fit nicely inside your larger marketing market. To increase your FBA Company, you'll need extra products in the future, so make a lasting, positive connection together.

Research Shipping

Those low wholesale costs will do you no good if shipping prices eat into the profit margin. Make sure you factor shipping prices into your general choice in regards to picking your provider. When sending products from abroad, there are plenty of rules, regulations, and taxation attached to transport, be conscious of how those could impact shipping expenses.

Besides transport costs, timely transport can make a difference in regards to goods that normally sell fast. Running from a product and not having the ability to restock it fast will cost you revenue, and that means you would like to earn sure that timely delivery is just another positive feature of your provider. Governmental regulations and rules may also maintain shipments, so make certain to plan sensibly and get your time down so that you will continue to keep your merchandise stocked.

Ship Your Merchandise

When you have decided which provider will supply your goods, you are going to want to buy and send your very first order of merchandise. You're able to send them to yourself, then prepare them to send to the Amazon Fulfilment Center, or you could have them sent right into the Amazon Fulfilment Center out of the provider. You'll have to follow Amazon's special guidelines about the best way to prepare and send your orders.

Measure 5: Establish Brand
This measure may be taken care of sooner in the procedure for preparing your own FBA Company, but since you'll likely have to await your very first batch of goods to be sent and made ready to market, this is a great time to focus on creating your brand. There are lots of steps involved with creating a special and identifiable brand that clearly defines you and also the product you're providing.

- **Organizing Your Brand**

You've narrowed your downlisting to one product or line of products, which is going to be your very first offerings on your FBA enterprise. But if you think about naming your brand, you have to expand your perspective and think about what your FBA Company will look like in five decades. What products are you going to be offering along with the people you are providing now? It's with the reply to that question on your mind you ought to name your manufacturer. Think about a new name that may more extensively cover these brands.

• Brainstorm many names that can be a fantastic match to your wider business standpoint, that exactly reflect what you plan to achieve.

• Can Google searches your listing of new names to see if they're currently being used, or use applications like Namechck to receive a clearer idea about exactly what brand names will get the job done?

• Make sure to think about brand names that have an available domain also. You will possibly go right ahead and find that domain to place it aside for you if the time arrives to build your new site.

Think about the name which makes it through all them filters then consider picture qualities of the name so you can readily proceed to another step in creating your brand.

Produce Your Brand Logo

In case you happen to be a graphic artist, then it is possible to design your emblem around the name you've chosen. If you aren't a graphic artist, scratch out a couple of thoughts and get in touch with a friend or partner who's a graphic artist that will assist you. You are going to want to keep it easy and avoid a lot of layout intricacies and colors since the more complex your emblem will be, the more costly it is going to be if it has to do with printing it as well as the clarity it's going to have when it's scaled into a more compact size. Have a look at Fiverr for a means to locate somebody to help draw out your style or consult professionals, friends or family and find that emblem nailed down.

Create Brand Shades and Tag-lines

Apart from a new name and a symbol that you will want to make brand topics and tag-lines which make your new and easily identifiable. Here's an exercise that will assist you in nailing a tagline or slogan which may be wholly unique for your brand. See if you're able to name the name as well as also the thematic designs supporting the subsequent tag-lines:

- It is the real thing.

- Great to the last drop.

- Quick food that does not taste quickly.

- Eat new.

- I love it.

- Maybe she's born with it, perhaps it's...

- Just do it.

- Let us sit down and have a dialogue.

You probably did not get the previous one. It's a motto used by a little publishing firm based in the U.S. but connected to Colombia. Its emblem has got the Colombian flag because of its foundation with the shape of a steaming cup of java at the center. The idea behind its advertising would be to convey that studying is similar to sitting down and having a dialogue and what better way of using a cup of coffee.

This ties several different theories and topics together using a tagline. The newest name matches. You wish to consider within this wide outlook as you create your e-commerce individuality and character and also reflect your message via everything you do.

Copyright Your New Name and Logo

When you've spent so much time creating your new title and emblem, you would like to make certain to make an LLC (limited liability Company) and enroll your name and emblem. To do this, go to the U.S. Patent and Trademark Office Site.

Step Six: Develop Your Product Listings
You've created the identity of your FBA, and your goods are prepared with Amazon Fulfilment Center, so let us start to record

your merchandise or merchandise. This is where you need to devote the most of your mind power and imaginative resources. You've worked quite difficult at establishing your FBA Company for this stage. Make certain you produce product listings that won't simply appeal to your potential clients but may also supply them with lots of advice to generate a skilled purchasing choice. This is going to be a significant component that determines your income amount. Thus, choose wisely and follow the actions laid out under:

Professional Product Photos

Professional product photographs that reveal various, significant characteristics of the product are the ABSOLUTE MUST. Inadequate quality merchandise photographs ruin all the work that you put into creating your individuality and your picture. Inadequate quality merchandise photographs don't adequately communicate the worth of your merchandise to your clients since they do not convey the value you put in your goods. Occasionally you will find specialist photographs for goods available from the provider, but there aren't, therefore, hire a professional photographer to shoot some high-quality pictures of your merchandise to utilize as product photographs with your merchandise listings.

Detailed Product Titles

Merchandise names are often the only way to draw the attention of a client in their Amazon to look for your merchandise. Although you do not need those to stretch on indefinitely, you need to aim to put some rather apparent, specific, identifying information on your product names to attract potential customers for a particular item. Try an Amazon search on your product group and also look at other listings to understand how they record their merchandise. Ascertain what's too much and also a turn away, and what's vital to grab attention.

- **Compose Your Merchandise**

Even though you need your merchandise descriptions to be more succinct and a fast read, you also ought to make certain your clients get as much info as you can from them. Here are some measures for producing product descriptions which can sell your merchandise:

1. Establish your perfect buyer in romantic detail. That is similar to developing a personality profile for a publication. Ask yourself questions such as: What is his background? What exactly does she do for a living? Where do they reside? What type of house do they have? What type of character do they have? What are their aims in life? What exactly are the pet peeves? What do they see, see, listen, or browse to? What could you say to these if you can sit down and drink a cup of java in their table?

2. Read product descriptions from some other vendors inside your class in addition to in different classes. Assess which approaches attract one of the most and make an outline or template blending the best characteristics of many unique strategies and styles.

3. Establish your tone or character in a friendly, enlightening, purely professional, lighthearted, enjoyable, and exciting manner. Here is something which needs to be comfortable for both you and the client you explained in the very first step within this part.

4. Learn how to use exceptionally sensory phrases that stir the creativity and lots of action verbs rather than sticking to be verbs.

5. Make sure you change the starts of phrases or bulleted lists using specific phrases and words so that your description will not become dull and predictable.

6. Make sure you highlight the best attributes and advantages of your goods.

7. Expect a variety of doubts or questions your client might have regarding your goods. This is wherever your perfect customer description can help you a fantastic thing. Respond to all those queries and concerns on your description.

8. Establish your merchandise descriptions in a nutshell; simple to see paragraphs with bold names and a few white spaces between

these. This will permit clients to scan fast and focus on specific features and advantages they are interested in.

- **Fill In All Of The Appropriate Info**

Amazon's product description type is nicely set up for supplying every possible piece of information that the customer may have to understand to produce an educated purchase. Make sure you fill in all the spaces such as:

- Colors, sizes, etc.
- product measurements and weight
- guarantee info
- Setup guides
- Merchandise specs sheets

All these little extras can make a difference to some clients in regards to making the last decision to purchase your goods or to proceed with this of your competition instead.

Step 2: Marketing Your Product
If your merchandise listings have an attractive and professional look, then you are going to find some incidental merchandise sales only because your product is listed in the biggest marketplace on the planet. But to truly begin turning overstock and ringing up sales, you'll need to draw the eye of possible buyers to merchandise. 1 FBA adviser indicates that you will need to "promote the hell out of your merchandise." That is not far away from reality. This is the best way to start getting out the word that you're available for business.

PPC Advertising

You probably don't have the funds to perform Madison Avenue Style advertisements, which means you'll have to start little and use simple, cost-effective methods to market. Among the most effective methods to do so is via Pay Per Clicks (PPC) programs. PPCs are a fairly straightforward and economical approach to acquire a wider audience for your merchandise. What it's, in summary, is sponsored articles that pop up if someone is looking for merchandise on Google or alternative leading search engines.

When someone clicks on the website inside that content, also it brings them to a product list, you may pay whatever PPC business, you've selected a little charge for this "referral." The fantastic thing about this kind of marketing is that you are aware that every dollar you invest in putting your goods before a prospective customer. You're able to take matters a little farther and do PPC advertisements through businesses linked to a product and target qualified buyers to get a much larger return for your investment.

Utilization Platforms such as JumpSend.

JumpSend is a very useful tool that helps you to get more earnings, better organic positions for your merchandise on Amazon, and more testimonials for your merchandise. It assists you with automatic email campaigns, in addition to establishing discounts, coupons, and giveaways. It enables you access to more than 100k shoppers around JumpSend, which aids with earnings speed to your merchandise and raises rankings for specific keywords that you are targeting Amazon.

Elicit Plenty of Product Reviews

What other consumers frequently need to say about that merchandise is what helps somebody who's on the fence about purchasing to go right ahead and make that purchase. Product reviews assist in selling your merchandise. People want to understand what kinds of positive and negative experiences individuals who've obtained a product have experienced. Besides inviting and eliciting clients to post an item summary via your fulfillment files, it is possible to even invite people to test your product and write an overview of it.

You might need to provide some away or sell your product in a particular discount (this can make them a user, which also produces a large difference as it pertains to authenticity), to secure those testimonials. The longer you consume, the more appealing your merchandise becomes to prospective buyers.

Hold Away About Launch a New Website or Blog

We discussed subject and domain at the "Placing Your New" step. That would suggest that at any stage, you are going to want to start a new site or site to offer your merchandise. This isn't your very best utilization of resources and time whenever you're only getting started. It's much better to enter this expensive, time-consuming portion of your advertising at a subsequent moment. The disadvantage to articles promotion is you do a great deal of effort with a little, virtually minuscule, speed of return to your efforts.

As some prefer to state, "you've got bigger fish to fry." That said, if you currently have a business site or recognized site, then utilize them as a way of advertising. Maintain your FBA Company moving ahead rather than becoming bogged down in articles marketing. Hold off till you find some adequate earnings rolling before going into such marketing.

Utilizing Social Media

Since social websites are where the great majority of the potential clients are most likely spending their period, you are going to want to create use of social networking as a way of advertising your goods. Social networking platforms tend to create your product more specialists and also provide you an outlet wherever your offering could be shared between friends or that which was known as "word of mouth promotion." Here are a Few Tips about how to use Social Networking in your marketing strategy:

• Do not chase your tail. Concentrate on just one station at one time. Should you distribute yourself to lean, you won't do the job efficiently in any of those stations. Pick one, assemble it up till you get started recognizing yields from your attempts, and move into the second one.

• Build up your profile. Make it interesting and fun, drawing folks to enjoy, comment, and discuss the information that you put there.

• Influencers will help establish and market your product. Get to know people who have a good standing who tons of individuals are after in a busy basis. Give them free goods and make them bring an overview of their content.

• Paid advertisements. Social networking advertising is fairly cost-effective as it may be geared towards target a particular market or interest set. This leads qualified customers to a product list. Qualified clients are generally buying clients.

Remember that social networking is a twisted thing; therefore, placing all your advertisements eggs in one basket is not actually in your very best interest. Use it, but don't rely on it as your only advertising and marketing strategy.

Blogging, Vlogging, and Podcasting

Yes, we've advised you to eliminate this. But, when and when you do start your articles advertising campaigns, you have to do this correctly. Even though they are various media types and implementing your approach will differ in type from one to another, your aims are the same with each one of these kinds of content advertising. Here are a few tips which you can use to maximize your articles advertising plan:

• Streamline your articles, so it pertains to a product, its usage, hints, tricks, and comparison with competitions. Make your articles useful, enlightening, and simple to read. In case you need to engage an expert to do it correctly, it's money well invested. If you create product comparisons, make certain to build the worth of competing goods, then show how your product is much better.

• Connect to additional content suppliers and sites. That is comparable to what we spoke with utilizing influencers on Social networking. You intend to obtain their followers to get buyers and fans of your merchandise.

• Post using a goal and do it frequently. Hammering your viewers daily using drivel will not do the trick. A couple of solid posts each week that can be helpful and applicable to their everyday lives will.

• Do not eliminate all sales. As we just stated, concentrate your articles with one goal in mind. But that goal needs to be serving the interests of the audience instead of serving.

Buildup Your Mail List

There's simply no replacement for targeted email promoting. It's the absolute most effective advertising approach accessible to you, and you MUST exploit its capacity to receive your FBA Company off the floor. Constructing an email listing is vital. The folks in your email list know and adore you, your goods, or both. Where is it possible to find far better clients than that? Let us have a closer look at this particular aspect of advertising:

• AN EMAIL SUBSCRIBER SHOULD BE OF EQUAL VALUE TO YOU AS A SALE. That is emphasized because it's the mindset which you will need to form if you're likely to succeed at building your email listing. In certain ways, all these are far more appreciated earnings, for the reason that they are earnings that will arrive later on when you may need them.

• Make Certain to get email subscriptions out of your present Clients.

• Have email subscription landing pages, popup boxes, invitations, campaigns, giveaways, drives, promotions, and incentive programs to promote email subscriptions. The more innovative and competitive (in a lighthearted and enjoyable way) you're with obtaining email subscriptions, the greater success you'll have.

• Do not depart from your email listing to rust. Provide with them occasional upgrades, hints, discount offers, and new product announcements.

• Do not drown them into sales slopes. Envision yourself up to your neck in sales slopes. Your email content should be similar to your site content. It has to be meaningful and focused on providing useful info or support to your clients instead of feeding yourself.

Utilization Coupons and Exclusive Deals

Many of you have likely noticed the comic drawing of a set of shoes recorded for $100. There's zero interest in these shoes. Within another period, the sneakers are recorded for $200; however, a reddish line will be drawn that cost plus $125 is recorded in red under it. Clients are struggling to have their hands on these sneakers. That picture is sufficient to set the point that has to be produced here. Coupons and exclusive deals are an excellent way to improve earnings. It's possible to use the tools in Amazon or even use bargain hunter websites and promotional websites.

CHAPTER SIX
MAKE MONEY ON YOUTUBE

- **Measures on how to Earn Money on YouTube**

Measure 1: Installation and construct your YouTube station
Your station is a private presence on YouTube. Each YouTube account has one station attached to this. A YouTube account is just like a Google account, and also making YouTube accounts will give you access to additional Google products, including Gmail and Drive.

Create your account or use your present one. Insert keywords to help individuals locate your station.

You can add keywords by navigating into the advanced section of the Channel Settings. Ensure your keywords are related to your articles.

Your username may also do the job against you; when it's brief, easy to recall, and first, folks are more inclined to recall you.

But if you're using a Present account, you can continuously change your username by simply editing it in your Google+ accounts.

Establishing a YouTube channel with your Google account when you own a Google account, you can observe, discuss YouTube content.

But you have to create a more YouTube station to upload movies, comment, or create playlists.

You can use a pc or your YouTube mobile web site / Program to make a new station.

Here are the steps:

Visit YouTube and register in: Head around to YouTube.com and click on 'sign in' at the upper right corner of the webpage. Sign in with your Google account username and password.

Visit YouTube configurations: At the upper right corner of this display, click in your profile and then the placing icon.

Produce your station: below your preferences, you will see the option to "develop a station," click this hyperlink. Next, you are going to have the choice to make a private channel or create a channel using a company or another title. With this example, let's select the company option. Today, it is time to name your station and choose a class.

Developing a suitable YouTube station is not a huge deal; here is an in-depth guide to establishing a Youtube Channel.

You may be asking right now out of tens of thousands of YouTube Channels and balances, how can your station stand an opportunity to be viewed?

Well, you need not bother since this is one of those challenges our pupils have been in a position to resolve with us our search engine optimization plans for YouTube. You can find out how you can learn this simple method too, click this URL to find out about our modules and also begin by optimizing your YouTube station for the best ranking

Measure 2: Insert content
Attempt to upload material that's high quality and is not super long. (This choice may differ based on which sort of material you choose to upload).

Additionally, attempt to incorporate frequently and stay consistent with your uploading.

If your content is not good in the beginning, maintain it. Practice makes perfect. Attempt to make every video greater than the past. You may often know as you proceed.

Boost your articles by using a camera that is better or trying better editing applications or methods.

Additionally, attempt to enhance how items are filmed. Utilize a tripod, have a friend help you personally, or light your moments better. All of it helps to get a much better end product, which consequently makes it possible to get a better audience.

By uploading frequently, you're able to help to hold an audience.

Folks are more likely to sign up if you include content on a standard program and keep that program as far as you can.

Make certain to label your videos with keywords that describe the material, in addition to an eye-catching outline. These can help drive visitors to your movie from YouTube hunts.

Measure 3: Construct a viewer
Assembling an audience is essential to raising your monetization. You want people to see your advertisements to earn any money from these. There's not anyone key to getting more readers. Make the ideal content you possibly can, and they'll come for you.

Keep publishing articles and attempt to get people hooked. Send out your video on Twitter and Facebook; share it with folks. Distribute it everywhere online. Clients are crucial to becoming a spouse.

Socialize with your audiences directly by reacting to remarks and making occasional movies associated with audience comments and queries. Connecting with your neighborhood will attract more visitors within that community.

Assembling an audience is essential to raising your monetization.

You want people to see your advertisements to create any money from these. There's nobody key to getting more readers; make the ideal content you possibly can, and they'll come for you.

Keep publishing articles and attempt to get people hooked. Send ut your video on Twitter and Facebook; share it with folks.

Distribute it everywhere online. Subscribers are the key to becoming a spouse.

Socialize with your audiences directly by reacting to remarks and Making occasional movies associated with audience comments and queries. Connecting with your neighborhood will attract more visitors within that community.

Measure 4: Monetize your movies
To be able to begin earning money in your movies, you'll want to allow monetization. This indicates you're letting YouTube put advertisements on your video. This also suggests that you admit there is no copyrighted material on your movie.

Visit www.youtube.com and click on "My Channel" on your page.
Click on the link referred to as "Video Manager" at the top bar.
Click station and Empower monetization.
Get in 4,000 wait hours and 1,000 readers
Measure 5: Obtain at least 4,000 wait hours to begin earning cash.
You can decorate a movie since it arranges by clicking on the Monetization tab and assessing the "Monetize with Advertising" box.

To market a movie after it's been uploaded, open your YouTube Creator Studio, then choose the station drop-down and then click on the Monetization to market your movies.

Get examined after attaining 4,000 watch hours at the past 12 months and 1,000 readers

Upon attaining this threshold, your station is automatically reviewed to create certain it complies with all the YouTube Partner Program provisions and also their community guidelines. Youtube will mail you an option, normally within a week.

This can be the tricky area, attaining a million perspectives on YouTube could be a significant challenge since you need to master the legislation of participation, and you may secure these engagements in your videos once you can hook your audiences using our participation approaches to get visual contents.

Nevertheless, the fantastic part is that together with our class, you'll master this approach and won't find it tough to strike 10,000 wait hours to your movies.

Step 6: Establish Google Adsense
You can set up Google AdSense for free on the AdSense website.

Click on the "Subscribe Today" button to start making your account. You should be 18 decades or old to produce your account. If you're younger than this, you'll require an adult to assist you.

You want either PayPal or a bank account and a legitimate mailing address in addition to other info, so AdSense can confirm who you are and that to send the cash to. You acquire money per advertisement click along with a smaller sum per opinion, but it adds up over time. That is the reason the audience is essential.

And as you understand, this depends on your viewers; you are going to learn from our coaching the way our pupils reach their initial 1,000 subscribers that turn for their very first cash off YouTube.

Great right?

Step 7: Assess your stats
Here you can see estimated earnings, advertisement performance, movie views, demographics, and much more.

Use these programs to determine how your content has been resonating with your viewers. It's possible to change your content along with your advertising if you are discovering that you are not bringing the consumers which you would like to.

Measure 8: Market your movies elsewhere
Do not place your videos only on YouTube! Begin a site, create a Site, or place them on an additional movie or societal networking websites.

The more perspectives it receives, the better. By sharing the Hyperlink or embedding the movie online, you're raising the prospect of it becoming noticed.

Now, we've got a Present blog article on how you can get free visitors to your company (companies like Affiliate Marketing via YouTube station) using online directories that have no less than 12 million monthly visitors.

Imagine how much lots of people could boost your view hour on your YouTube station...

But, keep reading to discover ways to find this done.

Measure 9: Develop a YouTube spouse

YouTube partners are all YouTube members that have monetized videos using a high number of audiences. Partners get access to content production tools and may win prizes to the number of viewers they've. Partners also gain access to more community assistance and hints.

You can apply to get a YouTube venture anytime through the YouTube Partner page.

To be able to gain access to the strongest Partner Apps, here's a manual:

If your station has been at YPP: when you get to the program brink, your station will be mechanically siphoned under the new standards. You can examine your monetization standing in Creator Studio > Channel > Monetization.
If your station hasn't been YPP: Practice the four steps to combine the YouTube Partner Program out of the accounts at Creator Studio. As soon as your station reaches the app brink, you're going to be assessed to combine.
Measure 10: Boost your YouTube earnings with affiliate advertising "Affiliate Promoting" means promoting products in the market for a commission.

Thousands and thousands of businesses offer attractive deals to affiliate marketers that market their products/services.

- **What's YouTube Affiliate Marketing?**

YouTube affiliate marketing is the process of producing videos and putting affiliate links from the real videos (through annotations) or from movie descriptions, including links to goods you examine and use on your movies, which will monitor a buy.

If someone purchases your affiliate website, then you get a small commission to the purchase.

You may sell/promote others' goods as an affiliate entrepreneur, in which huge businesses, Jumia, Konga, Amazon, and eBay, to smaller businesses, provide great deals to promoters.

Also, as a fellow, you will find lots of affiliate networks it's possible to combine, and I've covered most of these within this article about online affiliate advertising applications.

Here are some tips to earn money via YouTube affiliate advertising

Merchandise Unboxing -- In those movies, you may start merchandise at a YouTube video, revealing audiences exactly what is inside the packing. Then supply the affiliate link to this item site, where it's readily available for sale on the internet.
Reviews -- YouTube testimonials are another fantastic way to ease buying stress and supply an affiliate connection.
Training movies -- Finally, many affiliates earn money simply by training audiences how to work with a complex solution, and then sending people educated prospects for their affiliate link.

CHAPTER SEVEN
EBAY DROPSHIPPING

- **What's Dropshipping?**

Traditionally, retailers maintain a list of the Merchandise they provide available, frequently buying these goods in bulk at a wholesale cost in the producer. Dropshipping eliminates the measure of maintaining stock, rather allowing the vendor to buy wholesale products separately then sell them for again online.

Ecommerce sites like eBay and Amazon let vendors put their listings before a massive market with nominal processing charges.

- **How Can Dropship on eBay Work?**

There are countless of goods available on eBay; however, did you understand that many sellers that are online eBay never really handle or maintain stock of these things they market on the internet?

Rather, they supply their products from another online seller, frequently at a wholesale cost, and listing the most sourced items within their eBay shop. Many vendors may use the precise pictures, product names, and descriptions supplied with their dropship providers.

After a purchase has been created, the drop shipper will meet the order by using their dropship business, which will provide and ship the product to the client.

Since the products are sent right to your clients, you since the drop shipper only functions as a type of middleman between the provider and the customer, sourcing goods in bulk and sell them at a fantastic retail price for eBay.

Dropshipping is permitted on eBay, supplied. The vendor promises delivery in 30 days of the conclusion of the list. Even though the delivery time and product quality aren't right in the vendor's hands, eBay puts full responsibility within their palms.

Anyone having an eBay seller accounts can begin dropshipping on eBay! You will want to start by deciding what products to market, then sourcing these goods from a wholesaler or alternative provider that may guarantee rapid and dependable delivery.

You won't find a massive return with just a couple of earnings; the key to effective dropshipping is quantity. Many drop shippers only web a couple of bucks per sale.

Factors like pricing, advertising campaigns, and time can create or break a dropshipping strategy.

The biggest benefit of owning a grocery store is that you do not need to maintain possession of the merchandise that you're selling before you record them.

As soon as you've sourced a trusted provider to utilize for sequence fulfillment, only make your eBay listings and choose if to post, the best way to advertise, and what cost point you believe will fetch you a higher quantity of sales and make a profit.

As soon as you've recorded your merchandise on eBay along with the earnings start arriving, your second priority is to construct and keep up a fantastic reputation with your clients by meeting their orders and immediately dealing with any problems that might emerge.

- **Dropshipping on eBay: Pros and Cons**

There are pros and cons to dropshipping on eBay instead of creating an e-commerce shop:

PROS

- It is easy. Dropshipping on eBay is just as simple as creating an account and setting up your very first list. There is no requirement to confront the hassle and expenses of preparing your very own online store or e-commerce website.

- Fewer requirements for marketing. Your eBay listings will be placed in the front of a huge number of internet buyers, saving you money and time on advertising, SEO, and compensated traffic.

- More Traffic for Less Effort. The larger audience guarantees that you make sales simpler and get the lowest prices to your merchandise.

CONS

- List Charges. eBay charges a modest fee per list (the initial 50 listings are liberated) and around 10% of your total cost (called a "final value fee"). Together with all the already-slim profit margins via dropshipping, these charges can quickly accumulate. Remember that the real key to earning money by dropshipping is quantity.

- Less Customization. Selling goods online eBay is a fantastic way to begin an internet Company; however, fewer customization choices for your store and listings may help it become even more challenging to stand apart from the competition.

- Frequent Tracking Needed. You will need to remain on top of your lists if you would like to keep the quantity required to earn money via eBay earnings. You will find online tools available, which could help you to streamline the re-listing procedure.

Finally, it is up to you to decide in which you would like to set the majority of your time and effort once promoting wholesale goods on the internet, however for several vendors, dropshipping on eBay is a straightforward and productive method to generate money.

Listed below are our best tips on how to set up a dropshipping business on eBay.

- **8 Tips on eBay Dropshipping**

1. Reduce Your Workload
High quantity is the secret to attaining a competitive edge and making money with eBay, as profit margins are inclined to be somewhat small, often just a couple dollars per sale. Online sellers attempt to market as far as they could in a brief quantity of time. High volume means additional work since you have to process and meet every record individually.

To streamline this process and lower your workload, then find goods, which may be submitted as multiple-item listings. In this manner, you will make a list after, leaving you free to look after satisfaction and manage returns when required. Make sure you place a longer period for all these eBay listings to prevent "should" re-list.

2. Maintain Control of Pricing
The rationale millions of internet buyers flock to eBay a daily basis is that the guarantee of receiving the very best price for those things they purchase. This is sometimes challenging to get drop shippers

since the last sale price can differ, and the provider charges a fixed price regardless of what.

Also, eBay listings demand a listing fee, a Percent of the last sale price (as far as ten percentage), which may cut into hasty profit margins.

Luckily, there are numerous ways to keep your profits. When searching for eBay, you have the choice to decide on a Buy It Now list, which provides your product at a predetermined price, which means that you can make certain you pull on your preferred gain.

Another benefit to using the Get It Now option is that the insertion prices are adjusted, usually for a lesser cost, whether or not you produce a single or multiple-item mailing list.

In case you still wish to permit your shoppers to bid on your goods, taking the prospect of a greater gain, you also can try placing a book price. That is a minimal price the vendor is ready to take for the auction item.

With book prices, insertion and final value fees will change, so make sure you correct your book price so. This attribute ensures greater gains but may be bothersome to internet buyers since the book price won't be observable to the client.

The best way to restrain your profit margins would be to place a high starting bidding that guarantees you'll pay your fixed prices. Make certain to factor in prices by the provider (such as taxes, shipping, etc.) in addition to eBay's listing and final value fees.

You can calculate prospective fees on your mailing list by assessing its charge calculator.

3. Ensure Entry
Thousands are earning money via dropshipping on eBay as it removes the necessity to maintain a list; however, this may result in some setbacks. Among the greatest mistakes, drop shippers could make isn't ensuring that the things that they list on eBay are still offered.

This error gets bothersome for Internet buyers, forcing away potential repeat clients and generating financial hardships for you.

Avoid the pitfalls of promoting stopped or out-of-stock things by assessing your providers' stocks often to find out what is in stock and what's going to be departing their shops shortly due to reduced quantities.

Collecting daily reports out of the providers can help you keep a reputation of fast and dependable fulfillment with your clients.

Bear in mind, your Company needs its standing to be noticed in the contest, and disgruntled customers can easily place your store permanently in danger of becoming shut down from eBay.

4. Make sure Fulfillment
You have made sure that your listed items are accessible; today, it is time to keep your clients happy by satisfying all orders fast and economically. Reputation is what on eBay, in which countless internet vendors are competing for earnings daily, so make sure you remain on course with satisfaction.

The largest challenge with satisfaction is that finally, It is from your hands. You may send your clients' orders into your provider, but it is up to them to trace along with.

If your provider is unreliable, then it is time to proceed and locate another item resource.

A trusted provider will not just remain at the top of transporting the things quickly; they'll keep you current about the status of your requests, permitting you to know of possible flaws or problems so that you may relay the data for your clients.

Problems will inevitably appear now and then, however, keeping in contact with your suppliers, and your clients will continue to keep any possible bad responses to a minimal.

5. Look out for Unreliable Providers

There are plenty of providers available on the internet, but lots of Dropshippers neglect to properly display or appraise those that they pick before trying to generate income on eBay. This error can easily backfire in the shape of late deliveries, and also poor-quality drop shipped items.

Bear in mind, the client is not going to a provider for what they need --they are looking for you to supply them with all the things they compensated for in a timely fashion and at the quality they expect.

Even if the provider is at fault using the arrangement, the customer sees you and can respond accordingly with negative reports or complaints regarding eBay. Services such as web directories may help you save time by providing lists of providers that can be pre-screened for quality and dependability.

6. Build Great Relationships
Gaining repeat clients is a fantastic way to ensure large profit margins for dropshipping. The real key to having your internet buyers to come back to you for future purchases would be to construct and maintain fantastic relationships with your clients.

Building a solid reputation starts with measures already said: ensuring that the availability of these things you record, functioning only with dependable, honest providers, and staying together with satisfaction.

When problems come up, react to your clients immediately and professionally. Stay away from harsh or psychological responses, even when an angry client is outside.

Bad feelings will vanish, but these scathing reviews will stick around. Try to provide every one of your clients a very positive experience possible to quickly develop a loyal base of repeat clients.

7. Time Your Replies
Much like all else in existence, timing is what. When establishing an auction, the very evening of the week and time of day may have a substantial influence on your earnings.

Timing your mailing list around peak traffic seems to be the most evident alternative. High visitors mean more potential audiences, which may result in making a purchase more rapidly and having a greater profit margin.

But, record through peak times also means greater competition, in addition to the possibility, your prospective buyers may not have an opportunity to bid in your list whatsoever due to slow website rates.

This is particularly harmful once an auction is all about to shut. It is difficult to earn money as soon as your clients can not get to a list punctually!

Balance is the trick to time your eBay auctions. Consider the best times to record your merchandise and to allow your auctions to finish.

One key aspect to think about is your target market: Who would be interested in your goods? When do these clients generally perform their internet shopping?

By way of example, Saturdays and Sundays between 4 7 and PST p.m. PST generally observe the greatest periods of visitors on eBay, however more tech-savvy customers might decide to prevent these times to make sure a more profitable market bid.

Consider who may purchase your product as well as what their programs are like.

Look closely at the background of every eBay listing to ascertain the ideal time for future goods. Look at if your products experience a summit in traffic and establish the routines.

8. Make sure Trackability
The majority of the time, making certain your eBay clients can monitor the bundle is simple. Talk about your UPS, FedEx, or USPS tracking numbers together. Where this makes it harder is if you send an Amazon order into your client, and this order has been sent together with Amazon Logistics.

Amazon Logistics imports are the ones that are Fulfilled by Amazon rather than UPS, FedEx, etc., and also generally have a tracking number that begins with TBA that's followed closely by 12 numbers.

The issue with those deliveries is the fact that because you want to login to your Amazon account to monitor them, your eBay clients cannot monitor their shipment.

Additionally, but eBay does not believe Amazon's TBA Monitoring numbers legitimate. In the event you have to show that a product has been delivered through an eBay client dispute, then you will not be able to since there's not any way for either eBay or the purchaser to monitor the Amazon Logistics dispatch.

The best way to make certain that your shipments are trackable is to work with providers instead of sourcing your merchandise from areas like Amazon, who have these sorts of complications. Online directories such as SaleHoo can assist with this by offering you lists of reputable providers.

But should you want to use Amazon as a supply for your eBay dropshipping, be sure to convert the Amazon Logistics TBA monitoring amounts into types that eBay believes valid.

To get a comprehensive how-to, keep reading to our dropshipping guide so that you can begin selling on the internet!

- **The best way to Dropship on eBay: A Step-by-Step Guide**

Step 1: Locate a Provider
A thriving eBay dropshipping company comes down to quality customer support and the perfect supplier. You may opt to supply local suppliers to locate wholesale providers online.

When picking a provider, think about these vital variables:

What will be the shipping methods the provider offers? Are there any choices for expedited transportation?

How long can an arrangement normally take to send? Providers that cannot guarantee their shipping times set you in danger of getting dissatisfied clients.

Can they send globally, or just to certain nations? You might be limiting your client base without enlarged shipping choices.

How can they run quality management? Inadequate quality may result in bad reviews.

Could you utilize their source content (specs, photos, and product descriptions) on your listings? Professional-style pictures and descriptions may provide a boost to your earnings.

As soon as you've chosen your providers, contact them. Inform them you'd love to be a merchant for their merchandise and inquire about their policies.

Step 2: Pick Your Products

This measure could come before or after step 1, based on what you would like your shop to be. You may already have a certain product market in your mind, or you may have to run some research to ascertain what's selling right now.

Here are some examples of the top things to dropship on eBay:

Printed Socks
Bluetooth Headphones
Organic Tea
Vaporizers and E-Cigarettes
Waterproof Bag
Sports Bra
Resistance Bands
Baby Carrier

For a complete list of the top items to dropship on eBay, have a look at these tips ideas we have researched for you.

Step 3: Establish Your eBay Seller Account

Setting up your account takes just a couple of minutes; however, there are a few essential steps that lots of online vendors overlook.

Pay focus on eBay's vendor information center, which includes useful links and tips for establishing your shop.

Pick your account name sensibly. Crude or offensive usernames may drive clients off (and violate promo username coverage), whereas clever or tricky names may lead to greater earnings.

eBay might expect a tax ID for vendor accounts. A quick Google search will let you know just how you can submit an application for a tax ID on your nation, or you can see our post on ways to find a tax ID.

Establish your payment procedure. These approaches vary by state; however, all U.S. vendors have to possess a PayPal account or even a merchant credit card accounts.

Set your profile page with information about your store and its policies, such as return and shipping policies. Detailing your qualifications and background can be practical for specific niche markets (electronics and cosmetics, etc.).

Step 4: Produce Your Listings

Utilizing the advice provided by your provider, create your own eBay listings for every single item. Factors like pricing, auction, and timing vs. Buy It Today can be ascertained through a little bit of product study on sites like eBay, Amazon, and other leading internet retailers.

Take a look at our complimentary manual for optimizing your eBay listings.

Measure 5: Manage and Keep

Now that you have obtained your eBay listings, then it is time to create cash!

Start creating a positive standing by satisfying your orders as rapidly as possible, and check-in with your provider to get a weekly or daily basis to be sure everything is operating the way it needs to.

Eliminate listings for stopped or out-of-stock objects and replace them with new goods frequently.

Respond to consumer complaints and queries promptly, and professionally, and also do your very best to make a positive experience that can build loyalty and encourage repeat clients.

CHAPTER EIGHT

FLIX ANF FLIP HOUSES

Wholesalers earn again by signing up a contract to buy a home from a vendor and then entering an arrangement with another party to pay the same property at a greater cost to get again. All rights into the initial purchase contract have been delegated to the buyer as well as also the new purchaser pays a "mission fee" into the wholesaler to get all rights to buy the property at the initial purchase price. The initial purchase contract generally comes with an "inspection period" that makes it possible for the initial buyer to back out of their contract, not shut on it whenever they don't locate a purchaser to assign their contract into. Many wholesalers don't have any intention of really buying the house and use wholesaling as an instrument to find properties for different investors.

Often, if a different buyer isn't discovered before the conclusion of the review interval, the wholesaler cancels the initial purchase contract (via its paychecks) and has down the deposit. Wholesaling demands little if any cash to be procured in escrow, and typically the wholesaler never plans to buy the property. The custom of wholesaling can be marketed as "No Money Down and No Risk" by lots of property training businesses and infomercials because the true deposit may be as small as $10 and frequently even the deposit could be returned in the event a wholesaler cancels the contract before the conclusion of the review period.

Some folks are of the view that wholesaling is a fraudulent misrepresentation because the wholesaler does not really mean to shut the land. Nonetheless, in the USA, wholesaling is legal, and many property contracts permit the buyer a review interval and any quantity of deposit that the seller and buyer agree to. Land wholesaling is not any different from wholesaling in almost any other business.

At a successful trade, the vendor is frequently unaware that the initial buyer isn't buying the house. Sometimes, wholesalers buy the house for money and resell the property for their conclusion buyer at another closing. This clinic is considered more expensive since the purchaser is paying closing costs to buy the house and also to resell the house. However, many men and women believe double closure to be ethical. [3] In scenarios where there are significant gains from it often is reasonable for your wholesaler to cover for two final prices (double shutting) to prevent asking a huge assignment fee in their purchaser.

- **What's House Flipping?**

House flipping is when a property agent purchases homes, and then sells them again. For a home to be looked at a reverse, it has to be purchased to resell. The timing between the cost and the purchase frequently ranges from a few months to a year.

There are two different forms of house switching:

An investor purchases a property that can rise in worth with the ideal repairs and upgrades. After finishing the job, they earn money out of selling the house at a greater cost than they bought it for.
An investor purchases a home at a market with rapidly increasing home values. They create no upgrades, and following holding the home for a month or two, they pay a higher cost and turn a profit.
We are mostly focusing on the initial definition of home Placing, supplying you with pointers that will assist you to opt for a house, create renovations, and market the wise way.

Is Flipping a House a Fantastic Investment?
Flipping a Home may seem simple, but it is not as simple as it seems. Let's be true: A home flip can be a fantasy or a tragedy.

If done the Perfect way, a home flip could be a good investment. Within a brief quantity of time, it is possible to make wise renovations and market the home for more than you paid for this.

However, a home reverse can just as easily go the wrong leadership when it's done the incorrect way. We have all heard home turning terror stories--those were what looked like a fantastic deal because of a home with a shaky base along with a leaking roof. In the conclusion of the afternoon, a home flip might not make you cash. It really could cost you tens of thousands.

If you choose to reverse a house, you certainly don't need to lose money. You would like to earn a smart investment and benefit from the benefits.

-

- **The way to spin a Home in 5 Easy Steps**

Measure 1: Finance that House Flip With Cash
House turning could be a risky undertaking, and it is simple to see why incorporating debt to the mix makes it increasingly dangerous. This is why we always advise that you reverse a home with money:

First, flippers who carry on debt to their buy pay attention for weeks, which raises the amount that they need to sell the home for only to break even.
Secondly, with debt to fund a reverse can permit you to act out of despair. If you cannot get the home sold, as an instance, you're most likely to decrease your cost and reduce your gain. Cash-only flippers may wait out a sluggish industry.
Let us envision at a real-life situation: You buy a home to reverse to get $130,000. You fund an extra $30,000 for renovations and also aspire to sell the home for $200,000 to maintain a wonderful profit. It seems like a fantastic strategy, right?

All appears to be going good until sudden fix costs of an additional $2,000. And renovations require six months rather than four months, costing you an additional $3,000. When you record the house, it sits out there for a month until you are forced to drop the purchase price and sell it for $185,000 a month after you shut and receive your payout.

Here is how that breaks down:

Marketing Cost: $185,000
Buy Loan: $130,000
Renovation Loan: $33,000
Estimated Interest Paid Within Eight Days: $4,240
Repairs: $2,000
Closing Prices: $15,000
Your Gain: $760

Do you truly wish to earn $760 out of eight weeks of a job? That is a home reverse gone wrong!

If you had flipped the home with money, desperation would not have forced one to market low. Together with the capability to wait for the slow economy and save money on curiosity, you might have pocketed a $20,000 gain on precisely the same thing!

Unless you can pay money, the fiscal danger of home flipping is not worthwhile.

Step 2: Know the Industry
A good deal of home flippers gets excited in their following job and can dismiss this glamorous side of the enterprise. If you do not have a fantastic comprehension of the current market and property tendencies in your town, however, you can run in the next problems:

You do not know whether you're getting a fantastic deal on the home you are buying. Dave recommends purchasing an investment property in 80 percent of market value, minus the price of repairs.
You can not accurately recognize the house's potential price. Your vision to your home has to fit the fact of this area and the capability of the area's residents to pay for the house you decide on.

You do not understand how to cost the home. If you have purchased a home in an area of only $130K--150K houses, you' want to cost your reverse at the end of the range when it is time to market.

So how do you have a deep comprehension of the marketplace that makes for a prosperous reverse? Locate a property representative with years of expertise in your town. Your broker will be able to help you target your house search to the ideal neighborhoods according to your price, funding for renovations, and desired gain.

You might think that home you found online sounds like a bargain at $145,000 and contains plenty of potentials. (Consider everything you could use this kitchen!) But when the biggest house in the area sold for $160,000 three weeks past, some renovations could likely outprice the area. And you would be stuck with a home you could not sell.

It pays to use a Realtor who understands the market, such as the back of the hands. And when you are prepared to market, your broker can utilize their wisdom to cost the home competitively, so you receive top dollar. Dealing with a rock celebrity broker can assist you in making a wise investment that retains your finances on track.

Step 3: Create a Budget to Your House Flip
Do not wait till after you buy an investment property to earn a budget. Know your cost range for buying a house, making any repairs, even finishing renovation jobs, and purchasing it until you seal the bargain.

Make certain to identify any decorative jobs in addition to any expensive overhauls such as electrical or plumbing issues. If you do not possess a background in building, a builder can let you know what needs fixing and how much it could cost. Surprise repairs may break or make a reverse, so make sure you do your homework.

When you are under contract, use your review interval to receive a home review and some other special inspections you might require. It is always much better to spot issues on the front as opposed to surprised down the street.

Measure 4: Purchase Smart Renovations

Dreams of glistening hardwood flooring, on-trend lighting fixtures, and fantastic kitchens using professional-grade stoves may easily make your renovations to escape control. That is why you must learn your budget upfront, and after that, make sure your updates remain on course and really raise the value of their house.

Do not forget that large renovations--such as kitchens and toilets -- may certainly break or make your flip. Take the kitchen, for instance. Following this 2017 Price vs. Value report, the average sum spent on a significant kitchen remodel is 62,158. The typical recouped is just $40,560. That is not the type of ROI that you wish to observe when you are flipping a home.

If you are renovating a home that you hope to market for $220,000, do not put $60,000 into habit cupboard installments, luxury finishes, and dream Kitchen Island! Rather, think about a remodel which concentrates on remodeling the present cabinets, including granite countertops and replacing appliances. You will spend less, using a ton greater probability of recouping your prices.

As you may invest in a few large updates on a flip, do not underestimate the ability of little tweaks. Matters like a new coat of paint, upgraded hardware, and fresh landscaping may create massive effects!

Measure 5: Obtain Guidance From a Regional Real Estate Expert

Can you earn money from home flipping? When it is completed the right manner, you can! In 2016, reversed houses sold for a median cost of $189,900, using a gross profit of over $60,000. (3) Remember, the gross profit does not contain the total amount spent on renovations and repairs. But if you are in a position to reverse with money and remain in your funding for renovations, it is completely feasible to generate an excellent return on your investment!

The key to successfully reversing a home would be to get it done with Money, create a wise investment in the sort of home you buy, select renovations into your financial plan, and sell it fast. Possessing a realtor in your group helps make all that happen!

Whether you are purchasing a house to live in for many years or to reverse in a few months, an excellent real estate agent may supply the industry wisdom and practical advice you want to produce a wise investment.

CHAPTER NINE
INSTAGRAM AGENCY

Ahh, Instagram. With more than 1 billion active users, it is unquestionably a social networking outlet (for contrast, the inhabitants of the US are around 325 million...!). Possessing a bigger Instagram after can mean greater revenue for your company, more perspectives on your site, and also a stronger community for your brand. But how on earth do some individuals have tens of thousands of Instagram followers (Psst, that this unbelievable instrument enabled me to bring my Instagram into another level.)? Now, I have 11 actionable pointers that will assist you to increase your Instagram followers.

1. like photographs in your specialty.
I attended an internet seminar at which Susan Petersen (CEO Of Recently Picked) spoke about the way she climbed her Instagram to get nearly 400,000 followers. (Now she's over 800,000!) She stated that from the first days, she'd invest hours enjoying other people's photographs each evening. Proceed and enjoy 5-10 photographs on somebody's account.
Additionally, it would also help leave a real comment and provide them a followup. This can help to get your name on the market and also enables other users to detect you. I would also suggest doing so mostly to customers in your specialty. How can you find consumers in your specialty? Assess hashtags, or see the followers of your favorite Instagrammers. In general, be true and not spammy -- ai not everyone got some time for' crap.

2. Create a theme for your photos.
Cool, so if you followed 1, people would naturally begin to detect your username and might have a look at your accounts being able to offer them something to fall in love with! I have found it actually will help to make a theme for Instagram. Write down a couple of words in which you need people to connect with your accounts. To get mine, I expect folks glean that it is glowing, artistic, and filled with love. Which words can you use on your accounts? As soon as

you've settled on a subject, try your hardest to adhere to it! A couple of accounts which are killin' it? Studio DIY, Wonderforest, also Jessica Safko!

- **How to Create a Style Guide for Your Website (Free Worksheets!)**

3. Socialize.
It is not known as social websites for nothing! Respond to the comments you get and also leave comments of your own on the others' work. Instead of something rotten, click like for "adorable dresses," attempt to leave real comments and queries which invite them to place more photographs.

4. Produce a hashtag and invite other people to use that, too.
This is a good approach to construct the community and get fresh content for your accounts. To start with, produce an exceptional hashtag (be certain it is not being used!) and ask other people to utilize it. It works great if the hashtag has a particular intent. By way of instance, A gorgeous mess promotes followers to utilize #ABMLifeIsColorful on all their vibrant, joyful photos. Once people begin using your hashtag (also YOU utilize that!), then you're able to repost pictures from the followers (providing them appropriate credit, of course!). Does this build a network by demonstrating your followers that you enjoy their photographs, but also, it provides you articles for your profile?

Strategize popular consumers to collaborate.
Think outside the box! Request another Instagrammer in your market if you could "take over their accounts" for the afternoon for a guest contributor. Instagram Story takeovers are a blast and will dramatically increase your next quickly. Or begin an Instagram battle with daily drives. Finally, consider fun, innovative ways to socialize with others.

CHAPTER TEN
SOCIAL MEDIA MANAGEMENT

Social Networking management is the process of producing, scheduling, assessing, and participating with articles posted on societal networking platforms, such as Facebook, Instagram, and Twitter. A social networking supervisor might be used through a brand, person, or company to reach new clients online or to enhance and preserve their standing.

Social Networking managers are pros at managing Social networking action, from reacting to consumer feedback to creating strategy about the best way best to attain long-term marketing goals by releasing original content. But, also, there are social networking management programs that provide you control over your strategy.

Even if the time is limited, social websites management services and tools can make the existence of your societal website a priority. And in case you are not creating social networking a priority at this stage from the match, you are in trouble.

Social Networking plays an integral part of the business landscape. Together with 3.2 billion individuals utilizing social networking around the planet, along with 11 new consumers each second, it is safe to state the trend has become an international norm. Social networking management programs and tools can allow you to get to this massive audience and also make running a societal networking campaign simpler.

Getting Started Using Social Media Management
Engaging with your viewers via interpersonal media is much more important than ever before. Clients interact with brands through Twitter, Facebook, Instagram, LinkedIn, and much more, plus they anticipate rapid responses and professional manuals.

That is where the social networking direction comes in.

- **Social Media Management Tools**

If you are dipping your toe into the societal websites' marketing waters, homemade resources are a terrific way to begin. These programs can allow you to handle your efforts with easy, comprehensive interfaces made for the most novice of societal networking supervisor.

Also, societal Media management programs are frequently quite cheap, and several provide free models to check out before buying. But if you would like to actually make a distinction on interpersonal networking, you are likely to want a larger ship.

Social Media Management Services
While interpersonal media management applications can help your business increase the number of your articles, enhancing the quality of your articles is at least as important in regards to engaging your target audience.

Fortunately, societal Media management providers are equipped with all the knowledge and tools to handle your social websites presence correctly. Through targeted mailing, sponsored advertisements, and a vast selection of social networking tactics that are far beyond shared understanding. These solutions may deliver your social website's game to another level.

- **The Vital Elements of Social Media Management**

If you hire a Social Networking marketing agency or take benefit of a vast selection of tools, you will have the ability to completely change your plan from drab to fab without spending a lot of or wasting too much time. You will be able to:

Handle multiple reports across different programs
Examine social participation
Program articles beforehand
Get detailed reports of the analytics
Monitor remarks and react effectively
Collaborate with staff members on articles
Much like any added software or support your company. Benefit from, the greatest objective of social networking direction would be to conserve time and increase gains. How can social media direction produce certain advantages for your business? Continue reading.

How Do Social Media Benefit Your Organization?
Social Networking management programs and tools are created to make advertising easier, which increases profits. After all, what is the purpose of paying for brand new applications or solutions if they are not likely to enhance your bottom line? Social networking management programs and solutions have a bevy of useful advantages that will reinvigorate your advertising and marketing campaigns and set your business in front of your intended audience.

Social Networking management will assist you in:

Save simply by scheduling articles beforehand, instead of burdening yourself by remembering to article at peak hours during the day.
Boost ability by submitting many times each day on a vast assortment of platforms.
Know your viewers by supplying in-depth analytics, which describes who's after you, where they are coming out, and exactly what they need from your company.
Boost customer service by producing an easy pathway for clients to ask about your business through social networking and making it easy for you to respond.

Take charge of your manufacturer's standing by letting you track comments and opinions closely and react as swiftly as possible, and foster invention by supporting innovative cooperation across new programs for every social networking effort.
Certainly, social networking management has advantages. But, knowing how it functions is just the initial step in determining whether you ought to buy one of those services or tools to your enterprise. So, what's the next thing? Price.

Facebook for business is much more than simply getting Likes. Type your social networking strategy now.
Get Deals

How Much Can Social Media Management Price?
Social Networking management programs and services change in prices. That is the reason why it's essential to buy a tailored quotation before deciding. Most importantly, you are going to want to have an accurate estimate of just how much social networking management applications and tools will cost to your specific scale and demands of your company.

- **Price of Social Media Management Tools**

Most social networking management programs bill by two major variables: the amount of account you intend on handling and the number of articles you anticipate scheduling beforehand.

Social Media Accounts

The attractiveness of social networking management applications is the skill to schedule articles for Facebook, Instagram, Twitter, as well as LinkedIn from one stage. But, based on the number of accounts you are searching to handle, the cost can go up.

Whether you are hot on a wide assortment of programs or only have six distinct Twitter accounts you would like to handle, be sure to understand just how much it's to include more accounts for your ceremony since it might cost you a penny.

Social Media Posts

The main purpose of social networking management tools would be to schedule articles beforehand so that you don't have to time your day out to reach on those peak hours. But if you are attempting to choose the "quantity over quality" strategy, then you may want to invest a small extra.

Even if you only have one account, a few societal websites management tools can set a limitation on the number of articles you're able to schedule beforehand. The more articles that you would like to program, the greater the price tag, so be certain that you take into consideration when selecting your instrument.

Price of Social Media Management Services
If you are looking to genuinely break open the possibility of a social networking effort, social networking management services would be the very best thing to do.

The cost is a bit higher; however, the outcomes you will see from these social networking marketing pros will be worth it.

Unlike social Networking management programs, these solutions provide everything from an advertising approach to paid advertisements to boost your general Plan on social networking. As a result of this, social networking management solutions vary considerably in price based on a vast assortment of variables, such as:

The dimensions of your company
How frequently You intend on submitting
The kind Of all solutions You need
That programs you Wish to discuss material on
The amount Of all analytics You require
Whether Or not you will offer client Support through interpersonal networking

CHAPTER ELEVEN
MISTAKES TO PREVENT

- **Starting a Company That You Are Not Passionate About**

Occasionally people begin a small internet business not just to generate income, but since they're enthusiastic about their products or services. Starting a company requires your commitment and devotion, even if profits are not large, and you want to remain invested. You will find there's much more competition than you expect, and getting profitable will likely be more difficult than you might imagine. If you do not have enthusiasm for your company you decide on, then the studying and earnings process will look like the company will stall since it is going to be more difficult to invest in the company. As an instance, if you're selling plumbing components online but do not care about the merchandise, it is going to show on your customer support, quality management, and several other locations.

To become more profitable, begin an Internet business you're enthusiastic about. You have to understand everything about the products or services you're selling. The longer you enjoy your company, the more effective it's going to be.

Struggling to Make a Quick Buck at Little Time
Firms --both brick and mortar and on the Internet Companies are not always profitable from the very first calendar year. Some small internet business owners might believe that since they have lower prices than a conventional company, they'll make gains in significantly less time. Many popular novels promise wealth and four-hour workweeks throughout the area of e-commerce, but reports such as this convince individuals they can hit it wealthy immediately online. Building an online business is not as difficult than it's in "the real world" and requires time, effort, and preparation. Even Amazon was not resistant to the reduction of gain in the very

first calendar year, despite being in business since 1994 and also using more than $1 billion in revenue by 1999, the site did not earn a profit before 2003.

Do not make the mistake of believing it's simple and quick to earn money online. Make care to generate the company the best it could be. Thorough preparation will go a very long way when beginning an internet company. Be ready to work hard.

Struggling to Prepare
As soon as you have dedicated to starting an Internet business, you still require a company plan that summarizes the following advice:

Background info
Confidentiality
Products and solutions
Industry standing
Marketing evaluation
Creation and quality assurance plans
Financial projections
Executive overview

Although a lot of facets of your business will evolve time, in case you do not begin with a fantastic outline, then you'll get lost fairly fast. Possessing a business strategy makes it a lot easier to pitch investors (if you search for capital) because they'll have a blueprint on how you expect to utilize the capital.

Offering a remedy to some Non-Existent Problem, rather than pivoting after you realize it
Among the most frequent reason why online businesses fail is that they offer you a good or service which does not fix any substantial issue. It might seem to be a fantastic idea at the moment; however, after some tests, you could realize that the problem you resolved isn't perceived to be an issue by your potential clients. You will then find you could have new leadership for the increase of the company to better meet customer requirements. This company move is referred to as a pivot, and it's been achieved by lots of famous companies, such as PayPal. PayPal started as a firm that shared payments round Personal Digital Assistants (PDAs), like a PalmPilot, however, changed to a global online payment method.

If your company is built around promoting something which does not fix an issue, but sounds like it may be more "cool," that's a red flag. Be ready to change direction should in case you're feeling your organization warrants it.

Dismissing Negative Feedback
When starting a new Internet Business, It's tempting to listen to your fans and dismiss your critics. It's fantastic to have confidence; however, ignoring negative opinions or criticism regarding "haters" is an error. There may be advantages to negative opinions:

You can know your clients better
You can tweak your product
You may develop top-notch client support
Consumers suddenly, in a manner, use online comments; 88 percent of customers place as much confidence in online reviews since they perform private recommendations. By fixing negative opinions, you show care about the clients' experience with your product or service and would like to enhance this experience.

Use negative opinions to turn into a much better company. Let your customers understand you welcome any comments, and provide them sufficient avenues to accomplish this, such as surveys or even a score system.

Not Becoming Particular Enough
Many companies aren't distinct enough to get some traction within their preferred area. If you and your opponents are all doing the same thing, then chances are you will find too many of you at precisely the same small business. Because of this, your target market might believe you and your opponents are indistinguishable and will create their business decisions according to their budget or time availability.

You have to think about what you can offer in the marketplace.

Are you apart from other companies offering your service or product?

What's Your USP?

By way of example, how are businesses such as Zappos and Warby Parker different compared to other online companies that sell sneakers and eyeglasses? Warby Parker enables clients to test their glasses at no cost, whereas Zappos offers free transport both to and by the user.

In case your answer is only "we do it," then you definitely may have to return to the drawing board, as your intended audience will not see the reason why they ought to select you. Producing your company unique in some manner will encourage customers to purchase your service or product, and keep returning for more.

Not Defining Your Target Audience

Who's your ideal client? The solution could be "everybody," but that isn't correct. Not every company will fulfill the need of each customer, and that's fine. The thing is to locate that you can use your internet company, and determine how it is possible to fulfill their demands. Rather than defining your target market, you overlook the chance to figure out methods to market directly to them. Your internet company will work better against bigger businesses if you discover a way to target a market audience.

Identify your market so you can know how you will work in the current market and the way to target your campaigns. Don't forget to include your intended audience in your company strategy, particularly if you will seek shareholders.

Giving Up Before Starting

Entrepreneurship is insecure and challenging, but that does not mean. You are not intended to begin an internet company. Fear of failure may overtake you, so be ready to hit a couple of bumps in the street. It's normal to feel like you're not prepared to begin your company. Take that: Michelle Zatlyn, the co-founder of all Cloudflare, an internet performance and safety firm, told Fast Business it required three years to allow her to feel as though heritage CloudFlare was that the "correct option."

Do not talk yourself from beginning a business or give up in your thoughts too soon. You are familiarizing yourself with like-minded small business owners and friends that will give you comments, help, and reinforcement when you feel like giving up.

Forgetting about Discipline
There are many reasons why being your boss is an excellent approach to do the job. Although it's a fact you could work on your pajamas, then take the day off to play golf clubs, and sleep till noon, which does not mean that you won't require private discipline. As your boss, you'll need to understand to handle yourself. To be efficient and productive, you could discover that you have to dress as if you're going into the workplace, or place in just four hours of work later hours to compensate for this sport of golf. Bear in mind that the Pareto Principle," the company principle that states 20 percent of your time constitutes 80 percent of your earnings. If you are not working on a constant program, they are not giving yourself a chance for achievement.

Produce a program that's ideal for you and then keep it up. The more disciplined you're with your own time, the more time you will put into your company to allow it to succeed.

Ignoring the Legal Materials
Some online companies may tack on the legal problems regarding their clinics. Each step of your company may need an important legal record. As an example, if you're checking to know which sort of company that you would like to document, you can not bypass the incorporation procedure, and it is a frequent error made by small companies. If you would like to make an LLC, then you'll require an LLC operating agreement.

Other authorized mistakes that an Internet Business may make may include failing to summarize what obligations a business spouse will possess, and also what rights into this company that they have. You're able to circumvent future mistakes over those problems using a partnership arrangement. Another legal problem some online companies may confront is loan payoff provisions. Even a promissory note will allow you to specify how much the loan is for and the terms of its payoff, and even when borrowing from family or friends. Do not make the error of believing that because your spouses or creditors are your family or friends, you do not require formal instruction.

Allergic the Competition
People who have expertise in conventional brick and mortar Companies could be amazed to discover there's truly more rivalry online. The identical thing which might have brought you to the Web is fewer obstacles to entry additionally brings other folks. Everyone can start a company, so you'll have competitions. You will need to examine your competitors to comprehend the way you're able to overcome them.

What exactly are they doing wrong?
Which exactly are they not doing in any way?
Are the costs too high?
Are the products exactly the identical caliber as yours?
As soon as you identify your opponents' strengths and Flaws, it makes it possible to know how to serve your clients better. Concentrate on what you could do differently to satisfy the requirements of your clients.

- **Selecting a Niche, That's Too Narrow**

The World Wide Web permits you to find a niche market and tailor your internet company to a highly unique subset of all men and women that want to know more about this market. But, you will find drawbacks to market advertising. If your niche is too narrow, you'll not have sufficient clients; therefore, it's all up to you to aim for a suitable industry. Several internet companies fail as they're made around a vague idea that the owner is enthusiastic about, and they presume that there are enough men and women who feel equally to make a prosperous business enterprise. It's very important to take into account the requirement for the service or product you're selling on the internet, and you want to research your specialty.

Google has valuable tools to make sure that your market is big enough to maintain a business enterprise. Use them! Go to forums, assess tendencies with Google insights for Lookup, and utilize the

Google Keyword Tool to learn the number of men and women are looking for specific key phrases.

Too Far Keyword Stuffing

There's a good deal of awful information online, which encourages online companies to front-load their sites with keywords. This stems in the first days of search engine optimization (search engine optimization), as it was simple to manipulate search positions using as many keywords as you can on the page. Things have developed considerably since the first days of search motors, and businesses are not rewarded for arbitrary keyword stuffing. Today quality material is king. Whether you're a blogger hoping to create it like a company or are only attempting to draw more visitors to a website that sells real goods, your articles must try to be useful, enlightening, and enjoyable.

Folks respond well to articles that are composed for a person's audience rather than to get an internet search engine optimization. If SEO isn't your forte, then contemplate using a search engine optimization firm to raise the visibility of your site.

Not Enhancing Your Site

Many first-time Internet Business owners do not maximize their Sites for customers, which costs these earnings. Consumers need a site to load quickly 47 percent of users expect a site to load two minutes or not. If your site is too slow to load, then however great your product or service could be, your clients will stay away. Your company website additionally wants a call to action (CTA) on each page. A CTA is a message into the user to do it immediately, for example, "Call today" or "Learn more" if your site does not incorporate a CTA, you may miss chances for a purchase.

The mere presence of your site does not mean you own a fantastic organization, and you need to make certain that it pushes your own small business and entices clients to reply to the CTA. Check a web designer and IT expert to make sure your site meets your conversion objectives.

Forgetting On Your Clients or Email List

Every online marketer urges you to begin an email listing the day that you start your company. A lot of men and women ignore this information, and people who follow it forget that they have an email list of folks who need updates on your company. Email advertising is strong, and it operates; statistics demonstrate that the $ 1 spent on advertising equals an average yield of $44.25, meaning your readers are the very best clients.

Customize your readers with updated emails, special provides, and other articles that can inspire visitors.

Becoming Too Isolated
It's easy to spend all your time online as soon as you're construction and running an internet company. But an excessive amount of time can be isolating, and that deprives you of new and support ideas. Do not neglect the community both online and offline, along with different men and women who've selected self-employment.

Attend conventions and meet-ups, combine a group, have conversations on the internet, and think about if you should seek the services of a mentor or coach.

Conclusion
The World Wide Web has created unprecedented opportunities for people to begin their own companies. In case you've got an idea for a company, go to it by establishing your site and familiarize yourself with best practices. Get to understand your opponents, research your business, and generate a company program that provides you a roadmap to continuing expansion. Bear in mind that studying not to do would be equally as important as knowing what to do. By preventing the 17 mistakes outlined previously will present your company with the best possibility of succeeding.

CHAPTER TWELVE
SUMMARY

At the start of the book, I stated that I want to talk with you on the resources and wisdom we all picked up along the way and provide you with a few shortcuts to greatly improve your internet tasks. We've concluded the exciting and illuminating travel. I am sure that you have been subjected to company suggestions that will bring you complete-time or income.

Thank you for reading!